# A Very Personal Leadership

## Colleen Mac Dougall, PhD

◆ FriesenPress

Suite 300 - 990 Fort St
Victoria, BC, Canada, V8V 3K2
www.friesenpress.com

Published in 2016 in conjunction with the purpose and work of:
Leadership for Life Institute, Canada
www.leadershipforlife.ca. The author can be contacted through this
website to set up university credits, workshops, and retreats.

**Also by the author:**
*Restoring our World Soul,* FriesenPress, First Edition, 2012; Second Edition, 2016

**ISBN**
978-1-4602-7848-2 (Hardcover)
978-1-4602-7849-9 (Paperback)
978-1-4602-7850-5 (eBook)

*1. Psychology, Developmental*
*2. Education, Leadership*
*3 . Self-Help, Spiritual*

Distributed to the trade by The Ingram Book Company

*Dedicated to all those*
*I've had the privilege to walk alongside*
*in my years of professional life;*

*I learned from you.*

100 per cent of proceeds go to the Leadership for Life Bursary Fund to support graduate research in psychology/pastoral care that advances understanding of, and applies a new lens onto, what lies at the core of our historic global dilemmas.

For more information on this bursary fund, go to www.leadershipforlife.ca.

"We shall not cease from exploration, and
the end of all our exploring will be to
arrive where we started and
know the place for the first time."


– T.S. Eliot

# Re-membering

"Re-membering" is used in the spirit of T.S. Eliot's work:

Time, meaning, and the infinity of Life weaves in us a deepening clarity
about what we first sensed touch and call us. As life's circumstances present,
we learn more about the nature and intent of this call—exploring what
it means, what it asks of us. We sense renewal and aliveness as we open
to how Life aims to return us to itself and keep us *membered* in it.

# Table of Contents

1    Prelude

9    "Personal Way of Leadership" as a Shift in Orientation

15    Early Roots of a Very Personal Call

23    Living our Truth and Staying in the Flow of Life

29    Personal Leadership: A Process of Growing and Re-membering

**Recognizing, Tuning in to, and Naming our Personal Call to Truth • 32**

New Understandings • 34

Skills • 43

*Jenny* • 49

**Accepting and Trusting We are Held as We Move into Truth • 56**

New Understandings • 57

Skills • 62

Influencing the Larger Dilemmas of Life • 76

*Kate* • *79*

**Being with Each Other in a Way that Challenges
and Opens a Greater Sense of Truth** • **86**

New Understandings • 87

Skills • 92

*Brad and Jan* • *97*

**Keeping Alive our Deepest Truth as We Walk its Path** • **108**

New Understandings • 109

Skills • 113

*Patrick* • *117*

125   Arriving at our Beginning and Knowing its Place in Us

131   Notes

135   Acknowledgments

# Prelude

Who am I? Why am I here?
How do I lead my life when everything around
me is changing and throwing into question
what I first sensed (my) life could be?

Such are the fundamental and eternal questions we ask of Life.[1]

If only we could know who we are, we could stop trying to achieve who we think we are supposed to be. We could rest. If only we could know, once and for all, what to do with our lives, we could stop anxiously straining to make that one right decision that will secure us. The anxiety in the pit of our stomachs would go away. If we could accept that limits are not Life's betrayal of our dreams but reminders to step back and re-member to something even truer, we could allow the pauses.

There, we might recall in our earliest memories what inspired us. We might see that, though the world is changing and circumstances are shifting, what draws and calls us to purpose has not intrinsically changed. We could simply return to the familiarity of what makes us feel alive and connected, and weave this into a deeper and broader response to how Life is addressing us now.[2]

To stop trying to achieve who we are supposed to be does not free us from responsibilities created by our choices. To have growing confidence in what we are here to influence does not mean we stop searching and learning. To realize that limits often expose deeper truths—about our selves, about others, and about Life—should not lull us into accepting limits that no longer make sense.

> *Knowing who we are essentially, rooting our personal*
> *confidence in a responsive sense of purpose, accepting*
> *that our lives can be less about progress and more about*
> *meaning and significance is to live in a way that brings*
> *us into congruence with the unfolding nature of Life.*

This question—about what we believe is the source and nature of Life—is the primordial question that then informs our understanding of our own nature and purpose, as embodiment of that Life. Are we inherently flawed and in need of some form of completion? Are we seeded with an original life force that seeks expression through us? Is the nature of Life a series of ups and downs to be tolerated and navigated? Does the world exist to serve us or do we exist to serve it?

Our answers to such deeply reflective questions will determine how we search for completion, what we open to or defend against, the mood and attitude we hold toward any one day or event—including our understanding and interpretation of those events.

In the end, it could simply be that, no matter how Life unfolds, a sense of meaning and purpose can still exist.

Willingness to sit in deep reflection, unwrap our beliefs and our selves to the core, and determine a *worldview* with the power to shape what we *see*,[3] what we risk acting on, and what we trust when sheer will is not enough to move a dream forward, takes courage. But even more, it is necessary work.

> *Continually re-examining our convictions has*
> *everything to do with how we approach the dilemmas*
> *inherent in human existence—betrayal, identity,*
> *trust, power relations, injustice, and the*
> *recognition of inherent dignity and equality.*

The work begins in our earliest being. Experienced first as an innocent attraction, we progressively sense it as a call to gather together all that we've learned and to know the deepest significance of that call in meeting what addresses us now. In its most primal form, this creative movement is like breath, like flow, weaving and reweaving the impulse to exist, giving form to what we feel spiritually called towards as a cause in everyday events.

It was the Dutch existentialist Soren Kierkegaard who suggested that our origin, our nature, is spirit.[4] Our destiny, our responsibility, our essential and creative urge is to know this nature in ourselves, to sense it and make choices that perennially open space for this spirit to live, move, and breathe a great work in us.

To know the presence of this spirit of Life, to experience its movements, is to be alive. To respond and move with its call to purpose is to work this early sense into mature form.

The question that accompanies any *why* we exist is *how* do we live this existential purpose in a practical way?

> *What connections can we make in the here and now that, despite contrary voices, convince us we are living true?*

> *How do we trust that meaning still exists when hardship and confusion seem to permeate our every day?*

> *When our partners in life cannot see who we are trying to be, how do we search together for a truth that can deepen what we committed to?*

> *How do we lead our lives when everything around us is changing and causing us to painfully doubt that anything greater exists?*

How we keep our daily experiences anchored in purpose, how we risk taking up our responsibilities in this greater purpose, how we make room for deeper connections of love and understanding, and how we choose what to lead with when life as we've known it fades, is profoundly personal. That is, we orient our selves to these dilemmas because of our unique life exposures—individual, familial, relational, cultural, social, and political.

In this vein, each person's journey towards what, for them, holds meaning and purpose must be respected. This does not deny that Life resonates commonly in us, for in essence we know a *shared inside.* However, respecting the unique contexts that shape us and the personal nature of how we then lead our lives reminds us that, in encountering our selves, we must humbly and without judgment encounter others.

Listening without assumption to the particular nuances of how we have been shaped and how we approach Life—personally, racially, religiously/spiritually, nationally—will resonate in us a greater or lesser sense of our common origin. We may seek deeper connection to that origin, or resist and seek abject separation. But we never lose our unique place in our origin; we only sense more or less harmony with how we live in it.

As we release assumptions that have *had a hold* on us, we mature in our capacity to discern, hold, and *be held in* what is true. To mature in this way, to see and know beyond our small self,[5] demands that we learn to stand back, observe and help that self grow into the larger nature it is part of. Use of the word form "my self" (versus "myself") suggests this position of standing separate from the self and guiding its development into its more expansive existence.

I sensed a call to write this book. My aim is to walk with you as you open and energize new meaning into your life. I will describe for you a developmental process called Personal Leadership,[6] revealed to me through my twenty-three years of practice as a spiritually oriented psychologist.

Personal stories will help you see what the personal leadership process looks like. I tell my own story. You will also meet Jenny, Kate, Jan and Brad, as well as Patrick. Each of us tells of the intimate prompting and often painful unwrapping of what reveals that deeper meaning and purpose in our lives.

We share how we began to see and trust what lies beneath the appearance of truth, to open to what Life is rather than what we wished it to be. We challenge perceptions and assumptions to continue to move our selves into their more expansive natures. You will notice moments of truth when we make connections and know either congruence or the need for realignment.

Space is provided for you to begin telling your own story. At the end of each work section, you'll see a *summative question* (in round corner boxes) relevant to the content of that section, with space to jot down your thoughts on that question.

Putting your initial thoughts to paper here will provide reference points for you to revisit later—to see and gather up those threads that shape your story.

Within the text of those work sections, you'll also notice three formatting particularities that invite you to slow down your reading and take additional space with your art supplies and personal journal—*reflective questions* (italicized and left-aligned), *wisdom nuggets* (italicized and centered) and *calls to action* (numbered, bulleted, and off-centered).

Listen for which questions, nuggets, and action prompts draw you personally. Pause, make art, write, practice, explore deeper, expand upon—move around in and find your own way to integrate those images, words, invitations, and personal insights that breathe new possibilities into your life story.

I'll suggest a few places where pausing might be helpful. But you know best where your growing edges are and where you want to spend more time. Using this book to support your own ebb and flow—of new understanding, explorative action, deepening wisdom and integration—is where I hope the book will become your creative companion.

In composing our stories, we want to notice and capture those moments when we are being opened, when the energy of Life aims to move through us.

# "Personal Way of Leadership" as a Shift in Orientation

*I will grow in what Life, my relationships, and an evolving world needs of me . . .*

There are times and moments when Life's presence touches us in a very personal way. In those moments, we become acutely aware of how intimately we are connected with the sacred and vital nature of Life—how nature draws us passionately to stay membered with our beginning in it.

We sense this touch many times through our lives. A thread, a personal theme of meaning, runs through what is called forth in us. How we sense this meaning, and lead from it, matters. Even in fear, it is resolving: *"I will grow in what Life, my relationships, and an evolving world needs of me."*

In this way, the act of leadership becomes more than a time-or-place-specific activity of organizing and carrying out roles and responsibilities. It is a development and expression of our personal will to organize our selves to meet what Life is asking of us, addressing us with, in the context of now.

Turning toward Life and engaging with what *is*, is a choice we make. Making those choices is easier when we see and trust that Life is inviting us into something more. We can step into the invitation.

In coming to understand this orientation, you might begin to recognize times in your life when you have sensed this call to reorganize around something more meaningful. And in realizing this, you may notice a shift in energy: *Perhaps my incessant urge to risk something radical is actually an invitation that I need not fear!* Expect that your new perspective will ignite questions:

> *What would be different if I were to say "yes" to what I sense trying to get through to me?*

> *How will I make peace with the things I've let hold me back?*

> *Am I ready to take that risk, to move, even if I don't yet trust what I know must come?*

I recognize how naked we become on the journey of exploring Life's touch and risking its invitation; we get peeled back many times. Facing questions over and over again about who we are and what we must shift in our selves is hard work. But each time we see better what aims to open in us, we can respond differently to what is before us.

The challenge is to allow the experiences of angst, confusion, disturbance, even happiness, to connect in a more meaningful way what we hope for, and what is here and now. Each of us dreams about our life possibilities, even if we don't know how those dreams will become true.

Personal and professional experience has convinced me that we never give up reaching for Life's touch, even when we are afraid of what it asks of us.

> *It is easier to trust the intent of the touch when it resonates with what we've already sensed needs to happen. We then try to accept that facing what is before us will support, not destroy, what is within us.*

Life also earns our trust when we realize that what we are being called to re-member will not hold us back from progress. Rather, in returning to what we know, in weaving it into greater significance, we discover deeper truths about what does move us forward—making the urge to resist unnecessary.

We progressively mature in our trust of Life's intent when we see how even the simplest everyday encounter can reveal the potential for renewed purpose. Life gives us many opportunities to hone our inner sense of what still holds meaning.

I hope what I have written in these pages will deepen your sense of what has meaning in *your* life, and provide you with skills to reorganize around that meaning. Possibly you'll find ways to invite others into your journey; it can feel overwhelming and intimidating to face questions that seem to haunt us more than liberate us. There is value in bearing witness as we walk those convoluted paths of our Life work. Having kindred spirits to talk to, explore questions with, and to offer new perspectives deepens and expands our sense of what it is that aims to move through us.

You will read my story in "Early Roots of a Very Personal Call." In "Living our Truth and Staying in the Flow of Life," the symbols of water and tides illustrate personal leadership as a living, breathing process. It is this responsiveness to *what is* and *what needs to come* that makes living our truth a worthy investment. It is *the* life skill that transfers and adapts to any situation at any time in our lives.

In "Personal Leadership: A Process of Growing and Re-membering" (the main work section), I describe in practical terms how we can engage with the call to grow in what holds true for us. "New Understandings" and "Skills" provide hands-on guidance.

Finally, in "Arriving at our Beginning and Knowing its Place in Us," I share where I found myself at the end of writing this book. This journey has covered eight years and three continents. It continues to be a process that profoundly deepens my sense of the magnificence of Life's presence—in me and in our global midst.

As you reflect on what your call may be, try out the skills and let the stories touch your own story, note what gets your attention and what that might be saying about where you find your self now.

# Early Roots of a Very Personal Call

*I remember the familiar sense of what*
*stirred in me . . . that I was part of*
*something great, a promise . . .*

The call to care about and connect with the creative nature of Life has been part of me from as young as I can remember. As a child growing up on my family's farm, I had a name for every animal and watched in wonder as they gave birth to new life. I loved the feel of digging my hands into the dirt to cultivate the potatoes that came out of the earth each harvest. This touched a place deep inside me, and I would become enormously content.

I cared about the suffering of my family and friends, and was drawn to help them be well. I experienced a very real connection to all that was alive—earth, people, animals, plants. I have nurtured that same desire to *connect with and care about what creates that fresh, deep, and expansive sense of Life* ever since.

In adolescence and young adulthood, this desire took me on a circuitous route through a series of relational and vocational choices. As a teen, I remember lying on the bed with my girlfriends, pouring over the words of the song Desiderata: "You are a child of the universe and have a right to be here . . . and whether or not it is clear to you, the universe is unfolding as it should."[1] I memorized those words.

*Even now, I remember the familiar sense of*
*what they stirred in me—that I was part*
*of something great, a promise.*

I recall my relationships with men being about me trying hard to make them grow in the ways I needed them to. Now, looking back, I can see why I was attracted to them. They were usually very different from me—race, education, culture, age— and gave me an opening to live on the outside where I felt I belonged.

My relationship to authority was similarly uncommon. On the one hand, I had been raised with a strong value of respectfulness and doing the right thing. Yet, I had radar out for anyone I feared would deny me my will to create what I sensed was right for me.

I don't particularly remember learning how to channel my willfulness, other than to excel and stand out in school. Nor do I remember sensing it was a good thing to question certain authorities—like God. I had this complex mix of respecting the sovereignty of God, feeling deeply connected, but finding few to help me trust that the God I knew was different from the one I perceived I was being taught about. This separation put me on the outside again, though I don't remember feeling alone.

The lesson that I couldn't achieve my way through life just because I willed it also came through vocational experience. I once thought my calling to care would be realized through a career in nursing—but I failed an important academic standard. That being my first taste of failure, I roamed aimlessly and despondently for a number of years, feeling disconnected from caring about anything in particular.

I made other career choices, and while they were somewhat consistent with the role of caregiver, I still felt, sometimes desperately, there was something more I was supposed to be doing with my life.

Around that time, I read the following words in a simple little book, *On Caring*:

> To care for another person, I must be able to understand [them] and [their] world as if I were inside it. I must be able to see, as it were, with [their] eyes what [their] world is like to [them] and how [they] see themselves.[2]

I was riveted by the words. They resonated deeply with something inside me, something I knew and valued but couldn't yet articulate. Perhaps this was what my nursing instructors had seen in me—bless them—that I was better suited to sitting with the person in front of me, drawn to understand their story, rather than physically dress their wounds.

These words about the larger nature of care freed me; they opened space.

*I felt brave, putting words to what I had*
*always felt was different about me.*

I felt the challenge too. Caring in this more personal way asked for a deeper level of vulnerability—not so easy, considering my differentness, which seemed to make people step away. But the rightness I felt move through me spoke louder: *Better to risk than to stay on a course that isn't mine.*

It was a turning point when I made peace with failure. Rather than feeling that *I* was a failure, I became determined not to fail my self.

*I talked my fear into a place where it could see and accept*
*limitations as openings rather than closings only.*

This realization—that nursing was not the best fit for my talents and gifts—gave me hope and renewed my energy. I recall a sense of sadness too, as if I had missed something about my self that others had missed in me as well.

It was daunting work. I had to keep figuring out what mattered to me and risk many painful separations—from family, from a place and way of life, from a long-term relationship that had sheltered me. But I held on to a deep sense that something more was trying to happen for me, and many things did start to move.

I uprooted my life and moved thousands of miles away from the old familiar. One day, I listened to a psychologist being interviewed and felt a new familiar—this could be another way to care and to help people bring fresh potential back into their lives.

I married and grew to love from a much deeper and more spiritual place. I learned to see how my partner also was striving to connect with what made him feel alive. Through the dynamics of how we came together, I saw more clearly our shared desire to be known.

I entered and then moved out of a religious congregation that held me and blessed my mission. I renewed my curiosity about what spiritual community could look like for me now.

With family and friends, I was more honest about my need to move beyond meaningless patterns. Sometimes this meant stepping back from relationships in which neither person sensed creative growth.

I think of my professional choices along the way—I was never drawn to what many were drawn to. My approach to my practice as a psychologist was not main-stream, nor even collegially popular. I did not invest in training or requests for short-term behavioural interventions when I saw issues were more deep-rooted: "Individuals suffer all the more from freedoms (too quickly) obtained because they no longer know how to use them."[3]

I often felt at odds with the professional requirement to assign a diagnosis of mental illness. It was in helping a person uncover their at-one-time-healthy urge and taking responsibility for maturing it where I witnessed their hope and healing come alive.

Eight years ago, I knew again that I needed to expand my care—this time, beyond the limitations of my professional office. And once more, the prompt came from a little book. That summer, standing in the Abbey of the Isle of Iona, I read, "believe in what you do and do what you believe in,"[4] and sensed the wisdom again.

*I was ready to hear it and live it as what resonated true.*

My husband and I packed up our businesses and sold the charming old Victorian house we had bought only five years earlier. I said good-bye to the clients from whom I had learned so much about care. I followed a sense that it was time to write and more intentionally bring my work into the global community.

The call to care and connect with the freshness, depth, and expansiveness of what Life is remains the same. But my sense of what that means and what that demands in contexts shaped by factors unfamiliar to me is challenged.

Questions about money, power, identity, and the balance of responsibility con-front and disturb me. Stepping away from professional income but still wanting to support lives I cared about made me rethink my relationship to money—I may have earned it but did not own it. I had to be a wise steward of it.

Supporting human rights in situations where attempts at personal power could lead to a person's death exposed any arrogance I held about what my knowledge and skill alone could affect. Facing the sheer magnitude of what was in front of me while agonizing about my limitations in changing the course of *anything*, I had to keep willing my self to face deep and disturbing questions about my very existence—including how to let what drove me, move in me still.

Working alongside Tashinga Women Trust in Zimbabwe continues to be one of my most tender encounters. Tashinga is a Shona word meaning "perseverance." The Trust's vision is to support the rights of the African woman and girl child—equal access to education, economic power, the right to inherit property, the right to have a voice in political and social decisions that affect their lives.

When I first connected with the women who envisioned this Trust, I was touched by their drive to break free of the limitations of their history. Listening to their stories opened and peeled back truths in my own history. Witnessing their struggles to live what existed beyond survival made me question what *I* believed was essential to living what mattered.

These women and children have become my family. I have never seen them as impoverished *someones* needing my charity. I see them as *the other that I am*. But eight years later, even these words mean something more. In caring for these others that I am, I must never think too highly of my own power. Rather, I can only bear witness to what is moving in their lives and reach in my hand. They teach me that I am *the other that they are*; they witness my life in a way that is often silent yet powerfully present. I understand now the Shona expression:

*Ndiripo Makadiwa.*
*"I am here if you are here."*
*Ndiripo.*
*"I am here."*

I am sometimes surprised at what I am asked to re-member, to relearn on this journey with my global family. On the surface, faces, cultures, ways of life appear very different from my own. And there are deeply held social assumptions and role identities that have been conditioned into us. These notions of identity create noise around what holds power, where hope resides.

I am humbled each time I realize how such notions are never dissolved; they must be talked out in a compassionate and truthful way. When I lead with the belief that we are all searching in our own personal way for what is true, I can be patient with the noise. I know these souls. And I am reminded—I am part of something deeply and profoundly creative . . .

# Living our Truth and
# Staying in the Flow of Life

At the confluence of where the
"river of our experiences" meets the
vastness of the sea's wisdom, we learn
that what is true, what keeps us breathing
and feeling alive, is not constant . . .

Many of us know this experience of being in harmony and alignment with Life. We feel at peace, somehow *right* with the universe. Often, however, we don't create the space and take the time to remember what it is that creates that profound experience of opening in us. To take this deeper look is to ask the questions:

*What is it about the nature and calling of Life that keeps drawing us to it?*

*How do we know what we are drawn to is true?*

*Why is how we relate to, even name, what touches and opens us so essential to taking our place in unfolding the greater story of our world?*

As to the nature of Life that holds such deep resonance within us, we are of this nature; we know the intimate nuances of its movements, its pulse. "The river's flow . . . 'untamed and intractable,' courses through [us] with primitivistic urgency."[1] We resonate with how Life ebbs and brings us into retreat, with how it probes, sometimes relentlessly, into our hidden places.

We know the angst of quagmires that seem forever around the bend, feel the shifting needed to keep the flow of possibility and hope alive. Experiences along the way of the river (opportunity, trauma, loss, culture, racial and national history, economic circumstance, education, early family messages and values, mentors who incite difference) shape what makes our sense of call so very personal. The way we weave these formative experiences into a deeper, more expansive meaning is our personal way of leadership.

*Remembering that the ebb and flow, the quagmires,*
*even the disturbances and incitements of everyday life*
*are part of the natural re-ordering of Life,*
*we can trust to move with them.*

And yet, even when we trust Life's pathways in us, how do we know that what draws our attention at any one time is true? Johnston offers a simple, visceral metaphor. Truth, he suggests, is what exists in that "third space" where "something becomes more alive, larger in creative terms."[2] Using this perspective, then,

*One way to know when we are standing in truth*
*is whether a choice opens us and breathes new energy*
*into us, or whether we sense we are shutting down,*
*narrowing our capacity—dying to Life.*

My husband faced me one day and said, "Colleen, I cannot fill you up." It hurt to hear it but reminded me that he was not the one who would polish the dulled places in my soul. I had grown sufficiently by then to be able to hold onto my self and know: *I can open to this.* His limits challenged me to see my self in that moment and make room for Life to move something more in me.

To this day, particularly in my global relationships, I am reminded that I do not hold one right perspective that can polish the dulled places in a world's soul. Each time I become too convinced about the rightness of my own views, I am asked again to re-member what my place is in a story much greater than what I alone can see.

At earlier times in my development, I might not have been able to meet these tasks—hold my self long enough to sort through all the voices and layers of truth about what I needed, be patient with a sense of rightness yet to be revealed. Early learning—that God was sovereign but also authoritative—would not have made it easy to trust that God to hold *me*. History remains inundated with distorted needs to have *our* sense of rightness mirrored back—leaving little room to discern together what more could be true.

Taking the time and space to sense what is trying to shift us into another place is about staying in the flow of the larger creative process. We will our selves to be patient with how all our pieces are weaving into their greater whole.

*"At the confluence of the river into the sea, one*
*constantly influencing and being influenced by the other,"[3]*
*there is a natural rhythm that enfolds smaller meaning*
*into the larger body of significance.*

At this confluence, where the river of our experiences meets the vastness of the sea's expansive wisdom, we learn that what is true, what keeps us breathing and feeling alive, is not constant. The sea washes onto the beach debris from earlier ways of being, for us to inspect and reflect upon.[4] We sort through what in our histories continues to have meaning. We release back what no longer has Life in it. We open to see what deeper meaning can surface if we let go of our need to instruct Life— rather, allow it to transform us.

There is a familiar thread to what remains true, yet our grasp of that thread must allow movement, for Life itself exists in flux, in ceaseless flow. The famous and much-loved English poet T.S. Eliot, in "Little Gidding," the final poem in his *Four Quartets,* expresses this sentiment about the eternal shedding we experience as we keep what has purpose, a revealing, unfolding, breathing Life process:

COLLEEN MAC DOUGALL

. . . And what you thought you came for
Is only a shell, a husk of meaning
From which the purpose breaks only when it is fulfilled
If at all. Either you had no purpose
Or the purpose is beyond the end you figured
And is altered in fulfillment.[5]

Staying connected to this flow and to the lifelong pursuit of what is true, what has meaning, keeps our way of leading purposeful. What once served us well, may no longer. What before gave us a sense of expansiveness, may still seek expansiveness for what aims to come next.

We want to take notice of these inner signals. We don't want to miss those times and moments when Life is inviting us to grow into who we are and why we are here.

It is this deepening and expanding sense of (our) identity, (our) purpose that prepares us to take our place in evolving a world where competing forms of identity and purpose persist. Knowing better our unique place, the urge to have our gifts affirmed from the outside in is replaced by a desire to share and to contribute from the inside out. We no longer wait for someone (a spouse, a supporter, the CEO) or something (the government, the market) to provide all the conditions for growth.

Our world is undergoing a deep shift. Developing "inner leaders" who are conscious of what is truly before them and capable of uprooting assumptions, childlike notions and viewpoints is to champion (vs. violate) the common good. These persons are engaged, ready to act to help open the world to its potential.

# Personal Leadership: A Process of Growing and Re-membering

*Living in relationship with Life's presence is an oscillating flow . . .*

Living in relationship with Life's presence and sensing how it can shape the way we lead is a process of staying aligned as the circumstances and stages of daily life address us.

It is an oscillating flow as our "in-needness . . . urges us to be constantly monitoring our own personal interaction between our inner and outer worlds."[1] The aim is to make these inner, sustaining movements so that what is before us is allowed to touch and shape new meaning in us. It is our deepest commitment to "being the change [we] want to see in the world."[2]

Making these aligning, inner movements as the "in-needness" of our inner and outer worlds converge is the work of personal leadership. We sense fresh energy enter our lives as we:

1. Recognize, tune in to, and name that which aims to get our attention and open us to a deeper and more expansive sense of truth;

2. Accept and trust that risking truth will work a great purpose through us. We become clear on what or who in our selves is presently doing the leading (e.g., fear or trust, small self or wiser self, an openness to what Life is or an insistence that Life is limited to what we perceive), how this is affecting our capacity to grow, what needs repositioning to retain the space to prosper;

3. Be with each other, consciously engaged in how we are being personally challenged to step back and reweave our values, beliefs, emotions, and behavioural choices to help sustain a sense of flow with what is at hand;

4. Evolve in our willingness to mature, to keep alive in us what has value, power, and what sustains a sense of belonging—to affect our relationships, our worksites, and the world in fresh and purposeful ways.

In the next four sections, you will read about how to begin engaging in this Life work. You may even notice steps you are already taking to lead your life intentionally, and feel affirmed.

# Recognizing, Tuning in to, and Naming our Personal Call to Truth

*We all have those moments when we sense that
something in our lives has just been touched.*

It may be through a kind or painful word, a person offering a hand or confronting us with a truth, an event that rattles us profoundly, or a journey that changes us completely. It may be in a moment of "hitting the wall" or finally seeing an old conflict with piercing clarity. Our response to these touches can be reactive, dismissive, and fearful, or they can be curious and intentional.

Sometimes the touch is subtle, at first, inarticulate—just a general feeling that we desire change and a more meaningful direction for our lives. We often get this sense somewhere along our career path. Other times, the touch can make all too evident the mangled dilemmas we face.

*Times of stress when we know something has to
give, periods in our relationships when we sense
something shifting and feel torn, stretches of
confusion/depression/anxiety/loss when we can't find
the thread in what is happening—these are experiences
where it is harder to decipher the meaning.*

We have to weigh multiple factors, and they all bare risk. In the later seasons of life, there are other moments when we know the touch of grace—we see that Life has, in its own way, opened windows we needed to have opened.

We have many such encounters, sometimes within the same day, certainly within periods or across stages of our lives. And typically, we just see them as the process of living day-to-day life, disparate moments, perhaps not meaning anything.

Bigger events may get our attention—a serious medical diagnosis, an economic meltdown, a war that calls us to serve but leaves our soul wounded. Even these remain separate from what holds meaning if we don't at least acknowledge that they connect us to things that we could make matter.

Sometimes we are afraid to pay attention because things might get worse:

*What if we are called to act sooner rather than later?*

*Will we be safe going to those places inside that are dark and painful?*

*How will we find the courage to face what keeps gnawing at us when we know we don't yet have the tools to make the changes necessary?*

Other times, we don't know where to start. Or boredom may have set in and become our chosen reprieve. Jack Kornfield,[3] a Buddhist psychotherapist, suggests that boredom is a sign we have tuned out and stopped noticing our inner lives. We can feel alone and wonder: *Who can we trust to invite into our very private fears?*

When we allow ourselves to ask questions, we are more likely to be curious about what we are beginning to acknowledge—even articulate what is trying to get through. Is it our job that is not working for us, or do we no longer fit the job? Maybe we are being called to do different work or bring more of our selves *to* work. Is our relationship done, or are we finished with what we've let it become? Possibly the gnawing conflict in our relationship is, in truth, an invitation to bring to maturity that which drew us together in the first place (e.g., vulnerability, respect for personal space, a passion for arts and the creative side of life).

Are we being called to a whole new way of living out what matters to us (e.g., putting what we valued—financial security, public esteem—in a different place)? These are larger turning points where we might completely uproot our lives from a certain physical place and replant them in a deeper spiritual space.

*When we get clarity on what the message of Life's touch is, we see where to focus our efforts. We recognize and start naming what needs to be reorganized to regenerate freshness in our lives.*

# New Understandings

For us to see the thread that connects in a more meaningful way what is touching our lives requires that we put those experiences into a new frame of understanding. New understanding comes easier when we stand back and take an observer stance—being in a moment and, at the same time, watching our selves in it.

We become witnesses to our lives as we:

1.  Re-member (rejoin, sense new meaning in), through a life review, what calls us to purpose;

2.  Pay attention to how situations can reshape us; and

3.  Listen to messages from our physical bodies.

## Re-member, through a life review, what calls us to purpose

In the section "Early Roots of a Very Personal Call," I showed how, through my own life review, I began recognizing what drew me from my earliest memory and kept alive in me a sense that I was part of something profoundly creative. I understood that call (one that has threaded through my life) to be caring and connecting with the freshness, depth, and expansiveness of Life. Coming to such clarity takes time and is not obvious at a surface glance; one may have to wade through much damage and distortion.

- Find someone you trust, perhaps a friend or therapist, who can help you listen to your story and get perspective on it.

This may be especially helpful if the distorting voices are loud, if they came from those who, instead of holding up a positive mirror to your tender intents, broke your trust and interfered by projecting their own self-doubts and expectations onto you. You may have been told:

*"You are stupid to be doing what you're doing."*

*"You are never going to amount to anything."*

*"You have to be perfect so best not risk anything creative."*

I certainly recall the confusion of bouncing between messages that I was caring too much or too removed from what was "normal" around me.

*The reality is that we are often taught not to trust our own developing senses.*

Or, what if we trust what we sense is right and something painful happens?

For myself, I continue to get it—caring and connecting is living that delicate balance between standing back and stepping into what is before me—using what *is* in my power to affect that promise I knew about even as a child. But there have been many heart-wrenching lessons along the way. These painful moments were softened when someone made the effort to help me recognize and remember what I am really about.

Just a few months ago, a new friend said to me, "You are a teacher, a poet!" Pure joy surged through that part of me so often criticized as "very deep"—as though deep were not a good thing. A kindred spirit sees what's alive in us and is not afraid to join us there.

So take the time to look deeper into what might have been true about you before wounding voices cut you down. Look back to your earliest and most innocent memories. Don't be shy or embarrassed about appreciating this innocent genuineness in your self.

- Look back through journals and pictures; recall the themes you repetitively acted out in childhood play.

I remember hours of playing doctor, nurse, teacher, but never a mother—and that has been the path of my care.

Another way to get in touch with how you've been encountering Life and sensing your place and purpose in it:

- Listen to stories and observations others have of you—just choose, carefully, who you are going to listen to!

Whatever you come up with is likely to be more intuitive than concrete at this point. Instead of trying to force clarity:

- Articulate what you notice as an energetic intent, a sense or a cause that you have always felt drawn to.

You will read examples of this naming of intent in the personal stories that follow.

A note of care here: Make peace with what you glean from your life review; don't shut down the process before you get started. Clearly, alongside the joy we feel in coming to understand what energizes us and makes us feel alive, there is the temptation to pounce on all the ways we've not been living up to it. Temptations to blame others for our lack of progress or quickly give in to "I don't know" are too easy and distract us.

We have to garner the courage to put our past choices under a developmental and compassionate lens, even as we get ready to make different choices.

*What are my earliest memories of feeling alive and energized, drawn to a particular interest in Life?*

## Pay attention to how situations can reshape us

A second way Life calls us to live what is true is through insights catalyzed by particular situations. These situations may be one-time, short-lived events. They may be periods of time during which we need multiple exposures and longer stretches to become clear about what we sense. We may intentionally choose the situations or they may come to us—our only choice is in how to respond.

- A one-time, short-lived catalyst might be our participation in a sacred ceremony or a pilgrimage that moved something deep within us.

We wake up to what we really want to be doing with our lives.

My journey to visit places in the English countryside that inspired T.S Eliot's writings[4] touched in me a soul-stirring sense of what it means to return.

> *Immersing my self in the movements and seasons*
> *of nature—fire, water, air, earth—I felt renewed.*
> *Those same movements and seasons existed in my own life.*

That I was there at a time of transition in my life—stepping away from a particular way of work and opening to another—deepened the meaning of the encounter. Wherever my writing and global intents took me, I knew I had made the right choice. Something more *would* move.

- Reading simple but powerful words can be enough to bolster what we know.

Something unlocks, and finally we are ready to act. These are the words that leap from the pages of our favorite books. We furiously underline these words and phrases. They arouse and encourage something in us that had been formless—waiting for someone or something to give it expression!

Our own words, from scratchings in our personal journals, may bring us back to attention. We remember what we've been saying to ourselves—perhaps for a long time now.

- Multiple-exposure or longer-term experiences might include an educational endeavour that brings out a talent we hadn't been encouraged to trust or express before. It might be drawn-out pain from a divorce or loss of a beloved spouse/life partner that strips away what we hoped Life would be.

We might have begun in one field of study, one we thought or were told we'd be good at, but end up in a totally different field. Letting go of those we committed our hearts to, built dreams with, cuts deep. We can feel broken.

Finding new ways to express our talents, to love and to live again, comforts us: *Be of courage; stay open to what may be around the bend.* We have not been broken, only reshaped by the way of the river. It can take a series of attempts and even unexpected openings before it finally feels right again.

Other situational reminders of what is trying to emerge might be a visit back to our parents' home and becoming aware that we no longer invest in beliefs or practices we were raised with—that we align with something beyond that now.

- A new country or culture where we meet that which does not seem like us, rape or abuse of any kind, a comment from an old friend about a change they see in us, noticing within one self that something has shifted—all of these experiences, uncomfortable or devastating, if listened to, can open a deeper sense of what means the most to us, and the importance now of living congruently with that.

What situations in my life have shaped how I've
been living (or not) what is true for me?

## Listen to messages from our bodies

A third way we hear the call to live what is true is much more immediate and sensate. The message comes from inside our physical bodies—reservoirs of sometimes untapped or trapped wisdom.

- Thoughts like "There has to be more to life than this" signal we are entering a time in life when we want more meaning.

- Feelings like joy in our hearts and energy flowing through our whole being signal a sense of alignment with what we hold true—we are being expanded by Life.

- Anxiety in the pits of our stomachs, tension and stress in our heads and backs—these feelings suggest that something needs rebalancing.

When we act on what we believe, we experience congruence and peace. We feel out of sorts, having lost our way when we act against what is true for us.

I too seek peace and congruence; they are easier to stay with, even if fleeting. We don't like uncomfortable sensations. We avoid (addictive behaviour), project ("I wouldn't have done that if you hadn't . . . "), minimize ("It's nothing really"), rationalize ("I can't risk that because others need me to stay where I am").

*Defensive reactions simply mean we are trying to stay safe*
*and in control for the moment. But when defensiveness sets in*
*and takes over our bodies, this is a flag that something is trying to*
*happen, and it needs attending to if it is to be directed wisely.*

What do I sense my body has been telling me, perhaps for some time now? Am I willing to take the time to listen?

# Skills

Two practical skills help build on this stance of witness, achieve clarity in our life review, sense meaning in situations, and read the messages from our body. They have to do with learning how to *relate* to what we notice. In nurturing, even reconstructing, these positive inner relations, we feel a special kindredness with our selves; we shift to a greater source of attachment. The work is to:

1. Clarify what is ours to own and shift our direction of attachment, and

2. Create inner conversations that move us forward.

## Clarify what is ours and shift our direction of attachment

Securing the space to grow requires the skill of separating from anything that shuts down truth.

- Stand back and clarify issues of ownership (what beliefs and emotions belong to whom; where distortions are coming from) so that you can disengage from reactions and patterns (your own and others') that no longer affirm, and instead take the observing view.

We may not yet feel capable of changing what we observe, but just noticing our selves and others in those moments can be enough to shift our energy and center of power. We might seek out the support of a trusted objective party to help us depersonalize what is happening.

Depersonalizing a situation doesn't stop us from thinking about it or feeling it. Nor does it mean avoiding responsibility for our part in the situation. It is more about being able to stop reacting long enough to create the space we need to sort out what is really happening.

Having a boundary allows us to name and separate out what belongs where, what is true, what opens space and generates a sense of aliveness, and what doesn't.

*When someone doesn't respond in the way we hoped, does that mean we've been rejected or that we have not yet found a basis for connection?*

*Are we really angry at a situation or just using anger to cover vulnerability?*

*Do we really believe our partner is unwilling to love us, or is the truth that both of us are learning about what love asks?*

These are probing questions; our tendency is to hide from them and become defensive. But each time we find the courage to stand back enough to examine what is underneath what we thought was true—and what is underneath that—we get closer to a truth that opens space for each one of us and the relationship to grow.

- Bring attention to your boundary by visualizing a line of some sort (e.g., a fence, rose hedge, energy field) that fits with how you want your space to be defined. (Pause and illustrate as an art piece if you like).

Inside the boundary, we have ownership of our values, beliefs, emotions, and choices.

*A healthy boundary is one that allows us to be seen*
*and for us to see others without anyone losing*
*their ground and power to choose.*

It does not artificially separate us from humanity; it gives us the space to direct how we will participate in that humanity.

The skill of disengaging just enough to get perspective requires a great deal of patience and practice to learn because the undisciplined small self resists attaching to a presence beyond the idealized mother or father. This is especially true if we have had repeated exposure to damaging messages or traumatizing abuse—survival means locking away healthy needs for security, affirmation, and belonging in our "shadow."[5] We can become so frozen in that shadow we forget that Life still exists in it.

The good news about this self-imposed confinement is that it is a way for our vulnerable needs to stay tucked inside until a safer way to connect becomes possible. The tragedy is that, if too much time passes and protection becomes a hardened barrier, our needs try to survive by projecting and objectifying onto another the hope that, finally, someone (loved ones, work and government authorities, society) will meet them.

Our whole systemization of criminal behaviour and mental illness provides a way to codify, manage, and treat what has psychologically become locked away—disordered. But when we search for the cause and endeavor to heal the wounds of this deep and prolonged pain, it is possible to find the thread of what is still trying to live in it. Disorders can be ameliorated; we see their roots. We can redirect, re-energize, what has become sick in a way that takes into consideration all the needs coming to bear in a situation.

This growing awareness—that we must meet the world in a different, more mature way, that tucking ourselves away will not make the world safe—moves us to explore what place or space is truly safe and able to hold us when all seems noisy and threatening.

- Acknowledge and take intentional steps to explore and open to what exists beyond your human abilities and the ability of others to create safety. Study theology; be curious about other religions and conceptions of Life and of God. Try out different ways of positioning your self in relation to this higher Life force—notice what this brings up in you.

We search for ways to connect, reconnect, and re-member our selves to a spiritual presence able to hold what is greater than our human constructions of security. This presence is visceral; we feel it, we sense it move in our very nature. There is a sense of permanence and trustworthiness in it.

We return into relationship with it and re-member its steadfast capacity to hold us. Deeper trust frees us, intentionally now, to take that time and space to choose how we will respond to what is at hand.

Shifting power away from an external source toward an inner knowing, we are better able to avoid the pattern of replacing one addiction, one partner, and one job with another. We know an inner attachment.

When I get resentful, fearing that others are dictating my life, do I see that perhaps it is I who is resisting how Life is addressing me?

# Create new inner conversations

You need to trust you are secured in something greater than human limitation and, at the same time, realize opening to that trust is a process. You need a way to help your small self get there.

- From the position of witness, in the new space created by your boundary, build new inner conversations that both affirm and challenge.

When your fearful self shows up, pressuring you to not risk or perhaps over-risk, simply try talking to it like you would your best friend. Reassure it that its needs are okay, even rooted in something sacred, but it is time to try a different way to realize those needs. You are learning that new way.

- Choose who can best take on that reassuring role—your adult self, your wise and compassionate self, your sense of inner knowing or sacred source.

This adult/wise/sacred voice keeps talking to the fearful self until it settles down enough to prepare for greater meaning and security. Don't try to push your fragile self to do more at this point. Simply try to help it step back and attach to something other than its own fears.

This is deeply challenging work because fear has its own reasons for keeping us where we are.

> *The aim is not to deny or push fear aside;*
> *fear will not allow this. It is trying to signal a*
> *truth, however young or distorted.*

The purpose is to gain enough trust of the fearful self to help it begin to see what is possible—that moving in the new direction will give it the autonomy and mastery it seeks.

We can begin to use these skills immediately; we don't have to wait until we excel in applying them. We find our way as we walk the path.

When we start feeling Life move through our veins, we grow to trust its presence with us. Risk becomes more agreeable.

*Who inside me wants or needs to talk?*
*Is one voice more able to take the lead?*

# Jenny

Advocating for the disenfranchised, Jenny realized, was not just a childhood wish. It was also a deeper call to find new ways of being in her marriage and her work. When a situation overwhelmed her limits, she had to listen. By accepting what she could not change in another, she found a way to clarify and make peace with an inner place that was hers.

Her willingness to become clear—with herself and others—re-members her to a deeper sense of what living from that inner place demands in how she now leads.

Jenny shares her experience of taking hold of what was true for her, enabling her to use her position to make room for greater experiences of leadership to develop in her relationships and work culture.

# Jenny's Story

I am now fifty-two years old, but I still remember a childhood of feeling quite separate, a sense of standing alone. I have mixed feelings about that. I was an introverted child, conscientious, independent, and responsible. I liked being on my own and often sought this. I always had a plan and knew my place.

My parents taught me the values of honesty, integrity, and doing the right thing. My father, a reserved person, loved me without condition, and I knew that I didn't have to step up to any plate—it just was. At the same time, there was always a strong expectation that I would take the lead.

My mother was busy working nights and sleeping during the day. I took care of my sister, who was older than me. I'm not sure whether it was because I was smart or more independent than my sister, but there was a definite sense that I was looked to as being and needing to be more capable. I tried to please, hoping it would give me added value in my parents' eyes.

I liked school, though again, I was different. I was fast-tracked right from Grade 1. I just took that. In our family, there was a sense of being insular and steadfast. You didn't complain. You worked hard. You just got out there and did it! It helped that I had a strong sense of being able to manage on my own.

By senior high, I recall feeling even more different, socially awkward. I was younger than the rest, not at the same place as them—though I tried to be. It was obvious that people continued to have high expectations for me. I was smart, and you did something with that!

There was a split in me about this. Inside, I remember feeling judgmental that others were stupid; outside, I worked not to show it. I tried to not stand out for doing better than these classmates I saw as stupid—not to do poorly but to not hold up my accomplishments because it's what made me different. And being different hurt.

I'm not sure where, but somewhere along the way I became aware that instead of being judgmental, I wanted

Life review:
early sense of
what drew her.

to work with people, give them things, and make their lives better. I wanted to *advocate for and support the disenfranchised.*

No one encouraged me to be a doctor—though I wanted to be. (I had that whole caring ethic!) I didn't even think women could be doctors. Having a conversation about what I could do just didn't happen. I ended up applying to be a lab tech, but I didn't get in.

Eventually, I went into education, thinking I would buy myself some time to figure it out. I loved writing and reading, and saw this as a way to keep learning and improving myself. I wanted to be the best teacher I could be, so I took on various committee and training opportunities.

After the first year, I wasn't invited back. In my next position, fearing failure, I just tried harder to prove everybody wrong. I didn't have a concrete goal other than helping other teachers and consulting with them so they could develop their own skill set.

A situational
dilemma re what
most drew her

By my seventh year of teaching, a principal approached me about my leadership potential. Over the succeeding years as a teacher, I was asked several more times about my interest in pursuing such a role. Hesitating, because I knew I was more interested in human relations than management, I tried to put my energy into committee work that aimed to bring forth new ideas about how education could be done. When I finally felt ready, I put my name forward for a leadership position.

There were a number of subsequent experiences that shaped what I chose as my way to lead. My first year as an assistant principal taught me what I was not going to do. I was working under a person who was also smart, respected in the District, rising to the top, but who was very disrespectful to the people she worked with.

Hearing the
message from
her body

I got caught trying to buffer, putting on a façade of being this for her and that for the staff. I was taking care of her and everyone else, and it was killing me! I remember thinking, *I gotta get out of here!* If I wanted to be a principal, though, I knew I couldn't call her number. I felt that she didn't see the value of my way and would just say, "You're going nowhere." As a principal now, I see how leaders can get respect for things that aren't real but are more visible.

I began accepting that things weren't always fixable, that I was not always the one to fix everything. I knew I couldn't live that way anymore. It was during this time that my relationship with my husband took a turn.

**Clarifying what is not hers**

I was first drawn to my husband because of his differentness. He was interested in having a relationship where we talked—and he was interested in me! It was the first time a relationship with a male was not all about me fixing him. But as time went on, while he remained stronger than me at relationships, he struggled to get on his feet in his career.

**A message from her body; listening this time**

I was angry in my mind for a long time, thinking, *here I am again, carrying all the weight!* I wanted him to make money! We had come to the edge of almost not making it, but my new awareness that it was too hard to do it all by myself, that I was tired of being alone, I began talking. We began opening up about what we both wanted and valued. Ultimately, it was about family and the commitment to stay together.

**Clarifying what she most valued**

It would have killed me to take the kids away from their dad because he was a really great father. I started asking myself questions and decided that this was what I wanted to do. I had chosen this man to be my life partner, and I began to see that he was being true to that in his own way.

**Creating new inner conversations**

With my family, too, I worked to be less judgmental. In the end, I saw a truth in my self—perhaps I had been more distant than them.

This sense that I couldn't do it all by myself anymore became evident in my work life. I recall the time when an angry teacher confronted me and demanded more of my emotional attention. Acknowledging by then that I did need help, I reached out to other principals and a therapist to help me manage my emotions.

**A situational catalyst**

**Listening to her body's message**

I learned how to let go of expectations I no longer wanted to have control over me. I became reacquainted with those values of honesty and doing the right thing, only now I acted on them in a clearer way. I can't say the situation with the teacher was fully resolved, but I did feel

**Clarifying what is hers to own and to work through**

that I coped better, that I retained some of my own energy and balance.

Around that time, there was another incident, and I took an even more deliberate stand to do the right thing. Again, I had to draw a line of what was expected of me.

**Clarifying what is hers to own and to work through**

I was part of a committee with other principals, and one woman kept not showing up. At one meeting, a message from her was passed to me saying that she was ill and needed me to do her work in preparation for the very next day. I felt emotion rise up in me and knew I had to deal with it, so I called her.

**New inner conversations creating new outer conversations**

I particularly notice now how I have been leading differently, how this is opening up a whole new energy with staff. They are coming to see leadership as something they are already doing alongside me. I'm not the only leader here. It isn't my job to carry everyone.

**Life review: renewing her interest in the human relations piece**

Believing this has made me look for the leadership in them. I see more people wanting to be part of things we label as leadership now. They weren't attracted to a role where they just got complained to, where it was all administration—they just looked away when approached. I think now they see it as more about building capacity in others. A lot more people are really engaged in reaching the kids, genuinely interested in working together to help the kids!

If asked to measure how these shifts have manifested in the bottom line of our organization, I would have to say it's hard to measure right now other than to trust in the felt sense that we are moving from a disability culture to one of ability.

There is still that feeling I had as a youth of standing separate. I don't necessarily feel supported by the District in this new way of trying to lead. Assistance continues to be more about budgets and how many teachers you need—management issues. There is not so much help with the pieces that are most important, like building relationships and coming to a place where you grow capacity together.

Can you really teach that though? The only place this kind of support might happen is in our Principal Support Group. We often talk about things like: Who am I? What are my values as a leader? We can't support each other if we don't know each other!

I am also part of a new committee that is more involved in internally selecting new principals. This includes confronting the reality that, for the first time, applications are down—from 70 to 45. This is a trend, but perhaps it speaks clearly to the need to see and portray leadership in a more engaging way.

Having come to terms with the sense that how I am going to stay real and act on the best in me is up to me, I see now how that fits with wanting to help others see the best in themselves. I don't have to give myself up to make them do that.

I have chosen to take hold of and value a way of leading that may not be acknowledged by the District. But I see possibility coming back into my life and my marriage, and into a culture that I hope wants to find a better way.

Standing alone isn't all that bad because it now brings a different kind of closeness. I can see where I am standing. I trust myself to be here.

**Seeing what belongs to the organization, to own and to take up**

**Life review: a matured advocacy for her own life; standing in her values of honesty and doing the right thing**

# Accepting and Trusting We are Held as We Move into Truth

*If we are honest with ourselves, we might admit*
*we sense truth sometimes long before*
*we feel ready to accept it.*

This seems especially the case when we see that opening our selves to what is true will be painful. Becoming still and staying with what is clear demands we make choices when we can't know yet where the consequences of those choices will lead. We have to accept and trust that wherever our choices take us, we can thrive. We will not lose the thread of what we have built our lives around; our appreciation of how Life has kept that thread alive will deepen.

My experience is that space opens, and it is easier to accept what is beyond our control, when we come to a new understanding of what acceptance can mean and where it first comes from. We know a deeper ground from where we can allow what is, to be.

Typically, we talk about acceptance from a more situational context—one triggered from the outside. For example, we try to accept that something has happened, that someone won't do what we want, that we cannot make someone love us, that we can influence but not control how something turns out. We attempt to come to terms with these limitations through rationalization, weighing of alternatives, or just plain avoidance.

*When we see that our healthy need for acceptance*
*cannot be sustained by others, by a situation working out,*
*where we focus and draw our energy from shifts.*

# New Understandings

Growing beyond the urge to grasp for acceptance outside our selves, to labour for conditions we believe make life acceptable, is never an easy path. We've been conditioned to believe that we have to earn our worth, work for it—we must be deserving of it. We've been taught that we alone are the creators and holders of our destiny.

When we release these intensities—proving our selves worthy, believing in our own power to affect what Life is—we become vulnerable. We are challenged to:

1. Know acceptance as a truth emerging from the inside out, and

2. Trust that Life holds us and has a way to help us accept and move into what is true.

## Know acceptance as a truth that emerges from the inside out

To open to an acceptance sacredly imbued and internally revealed, we must first:

- Become still enough to sense this inner dimension of Life and allow it to make itself known to us.

We must believe and trust that what emerges from the crevices of our innermost being is of a sacred nature—that being of this nature, we are inherently worthy of acceptance.

*How we work through, peel back, our psychological wounds
and our social/cultural conditioning to open to this
inner and sacred trust will depend on
our life experience, context, and worldview.*

Our wounds may feel overwhelming. Early loss can leave us constantly searching for places to belong. Social, cultural, and sexual denigration weighs heavily on the soul that struggles simply to be allowed to breathe.

The injustice of oppression and a repressive rule that believes only in its own entitlement and view on truth presses in on our will to liberate a different view on how the world could be. It can feel like there's little room to recover or re-member what is sacred about our lives. We may not have been exposed to critical thought.

We also differ in how we make sense of truth, through what lens or realms of existence we know meaning. One person's insight may be initiated through reflection. For another, a powerful emotional experience may be what wrenches them open and convinces them to see who they are, what direction to risk.

Different religious and spiritual beliefs have a primal impact on how we come to know the truth of our nature, how we feel led to act on that truth, what words and ways of seeing resonate in us. Is our nature human only or is our human life a vessel through which a spirit nature moves and breathes? Our views on the source of good and evil pull our energies toward redemptive or ecumenical approaches to spiritual life.

Based on what we believe, we hold strong positions on everything from the nature of the criminal mind to motives for power—even what name we give to any sense of a god.

> *Individuals must retain the right to choose how*
> *they will open themselves to what they believe. This right*
> *co-exists with the responsibility for exploring what practices*
> *preserve the inherent dignity and value of each one.*

Trusting that we are accepted by a source beyond our ability to prove our selves worthy is to step into an invitation. For many of us, the invitation agitates the deepest and most primal of dilemmas. Convinced that we know best the intricacies of our inner world, what will happen if we become vulnerable to that which knows us in a way we have yet to know our selves?

To open our selves to this source, we have to believe that we are *of* this Life source. The invitation is to return and stay membered in it.

When we know this inner place of deep acceptance, we are more able to meet and work with what may be difficult to accept externally. We have a place from which to respond versus react when the noise of life says, "You aren't good enough." There is room to:

- Reorganize, separate out our spiritual worth from the physical situation at hand.

We are free to influence, without needing to control, the best of what is trying to unfold.

*. . . Be still and listen . . . Continue my Story*

*What values and beliefs have enabled me or prevented me from accepting my self as a sacred being? What experiences shaped these values and beliefs in me?*

# Trust that Life holds us as we accept and move into what is true

Realigning and allowing the sacred source of Life within to hold us and provide a safe place from which to move past old betrayals is a deeply transformative experience. It is a commitment that we make—again and again—as the circumstances of life weigh down our ability to see past immediate challenges.

- Know that someone or something greater than our fear holds what is possible until the conditions for growth come together. Space opens—often in ways we haven't imagined.

We need to trust that risking, stepping into those spaces, even intentionally exposing our selves to what disturbs us, will not separate us from what holds power.

Believing that Life has this power is a commitment—to allow Life the space to work in us. We begin to see why it matters that we respond (not react) to life circumstances to preserve that growing space. We accept that *being for others* means allowing and preserving room for them to make their own internal shifts and experience their own personal transformations.

- Let go of attachments that we've grown beyond and release others—parents, spouses, our children, employers, institutions—from the demand that they remain as we need them to.

They too must be free to explore what holds their reason for being—beyond our own needs of them.

We may not yet see what allowing Life to open and transform us can affect. But we can trust that if we stay attentive to what Life is attempting to shape in us, our lives will be expanded.

How open have I been to letting something,
someone, beyond my control "hold" me?

# Skills

How we come to accept the greater nature of which we are, and allow our lives to be held within it will be strongly influenced by what has shaped us up to now. Yet this need not be the final say on who we become. There are at least two basic skills that can help us stay with any distortions and manage early wounds.

They naturally flow from the skills of clarifying what is ours and creating new inner conversations. Here, we do the work of *remaining aligned* with our growing inner sense of what can make the difference as we face the contexts and dilemmas of everyday life.

The task is to stand back and keep realigning with what we desire and feel called to live our lives around (e.g., love, forgiveness, truth, service, care). Realignment is a lifelong process but we sense fresh possibilities every time we:

1. Befriend our limits while trusting that Life itself will provide the opportunities for what is to come next, and

2. Bring into congruence, through conscious and developmental choice, what we discern to be true.

## Befriend our limits

One of the hardest things I continue to learn in my journey is that I alone cannot care in all the ways that care is needed. Befriending our limits, while also trusting that Life will bring forth what is to come next, means re-membering that Life, and what evolves in it, is bigger than us.

> *A deep and very real fear knots in my belly when*
> *I realize my limitations. I know that dilemmas*
> *may not be resolved, needs may not be met,*
> *goals may not be reached. The fear is especially*
> *sharp because of early life messages to*
> *"not quit" and "be responsible."*

In facing any dilemma (betrayal, an offense against our personhood, feeling "robbed" of our dignity and our dreams), the choices are difficult: We have to get clear on who or what we are truly responsible to; we have to figure out how we feel toward, and what we believe about, our betrayer; we have to decide if we want our betrayer punished or if we will support rehabilitation; we can remember that no one can rob us of our dignity and our dreams.

The developmental choices we make exist on two planes—psychological and spiritual. On the psychological level, the choice is:

- Allow logic to convince your emotions and reactions of the futility of their singular efforts to make happen what they need (e.g., that justice will come in the form they demand, that the other will redeem themselves and give you both back your dignity).

This builds on our new inner conversations but takes them to a deeper level. Here, we work through those conversations to gain the cooperation of the fearful—even bitter—self.

> Fearful/bitter self: "In a minute, things can derail and there's nothing you can do about it. All because of one stupid decision."

> Listening/wise self *[nodding]*: "One minute you were driving home, then *CRASH* . . . legs shredded to the bone . . . son gone . . . dreams frozen . . ."

> Fearful/bitter self *[sitting with head in hands]*: "Nothing makes sense anymore."

> Listening/wise self *[looks to the grieving/bitter self]*: "You wish you could roll back time. You want him to pay. You want your life back."

> Grieving/bitter self *[points to the listening/compassionate self]*: "Wouldn't you?"

> Compassionate/wise self *[nodding to the lost/grieving self]*: "Yes, I would. Whatever that meant."

On the spiritual level, the choice is to:

- Accept that even human wisdom has limitations.

Turning to see those who have violated us as coming from a place of sickness, to see human circumstance as a wrenching open (versus betrayal) of what Life is, requires a very different understanding of what is "just" and what it means to lead one's life—despite, or even because of, the betrayal, the loss, the violation.

The questions we have to ask our selves are complex:

*Am I willing to see the wound in the other who betrayed me?*

*What belief will help me see this crime in a way that lets me breathe and stay open to what can be restored?*

*What still makes sense to work for and dream?*

Accepting our human limits—and those of others—expands our awareness. We risk opening to what is beyond our own capacity to control or influence. If we are to breathe again, we must find the thread and the dream we fear has been severed.

But there is an even deeper and more painful awareness that acknowledging and befriending limits can open. Something shakes us awake; we realize that in not respecting limits, *we* have become the betrayer—of another person/culture/race/ way of life, of the very values and beliefs we stand for. Our best intentions have become mangled, confused.

I came to this painful realization in my own life. Why was the way I thought I had been caring falling flat? My heart was wide open; I had held nothing back. But after too many times of battling this inner angst, I had to face the possibility that I was becoming disconnected from the very cause I lived and worked for (that each could know and stand in their inalienable Right to Live). Once more, it was words from the little book *On Caring* that touched me:

> If caring is to take place, not only are certain actions and attitudes on my part necessary, but there must also be developmental change in the other as a result of what I do; I must actually help the other grow.[6]

I was immediately challenged. Had I not stepped back to see whether my care was actually helping move something greater? Was it my place to respond to all the situation called for? What in me was driving this urge to too quickly step into another's life and assume I had the power to open the path that empowered their life dreams? Perhaps I had been judging and placing my own western template on their dream.

I continue to ask my self: What is the offering, the movement toward, that opens personal, cultural, and global space in a way that makes us want to learn and grow beyond what our fears think is needed? How we talk with one another and support that inner building up and unfolding can preserve the dignity of each one.

Any difference we make in each other's lives may be beyond what we can presently see. Taking time to notice what is already moving, perhaps despite effort on our part, will keep us humble.

What limitations am I beginning to recognize in my self?
Am I making peace with them or fighting them?

## Bring into congruence what we discern to be true

This deepening sense of congruence between our limits, our acceptance of situational limits, and our appreciation of what is in front of us requires staying open and allowing Life to teach us. It takes that deeper level of trust that "Life is unfolding as it should."[7]

Space is then available for the second skill: bringing into congruence, through conscious and developmental choice, what we experience and progressively know to be true. This is the core work of the personal leadership process.

There are four entry points into this realignment process: *re-examining values, reframing beliefs, processing emotion,* and *redirecting behaviour.*

It doesn't matter where you enter. You might gravitate toward what is getting your attention at present (e.g., emotional confusion) or how you personally sense meaning (e.g., asking what has value).  Perhaps you are at an impasse about what action to take (e.g., your behaviour has been confronted). You may no longer know what you believe (e.g., you resist what you don't believe but have yet to clarify what you do believe).

Move around in these four aspects of the personal leadership process outlined below.

## Identify and re-examine what you value

- With pencil in hand, and in the space provided, begin to name the core values you want to manifest in how you live.

Values are powerful motivators, so you want your chosen values to move you and deeply energize you. Many of us hold common humanitarian values—service, honesty, and freedom. Even these become more personal when we invest them with our own sense of why they matter.

We may, for example, value *social justice.* But in a world where the realities of social inequity and suffering remain, it is time to re-examine whether our efforts to "treat" the legacies of oppressive power are meeting their aim. Placing what has held power (including our own rush to impose solutions) onto a lower rung and stepping aside so that the other can rise makes evident the deeper and more spiritual value of *creative justice.*

Here, it is less about doing from a perceived position of power. It is more about making room for the other to grow, and for us all to know a different experience of our selves.

*What values are apparent in how I'm living?*
*Are they values I have chosen?*

# Record your core beliefs, including your belief about your true nature

- Dig deep. Make two columns if that will help you sort out which beliefs you no longer wish to hold, and which ones you are getting reacquainted with.

What we believe has enormous influence on how we show up in the world, relate to one another, and approach dilemmas. Our beliefs orient us to the world in a specific way. When clarifying what we believe, we want to make sure we are not just choosing what has been given to us, but what more essentially allows us to live according to our values.

- Alternatively, reframe your beliefs and give them a deeper context to reveal what they truly mean to you.

    Example 1: "I am different and don't fit in" might be reframed as "I have an uncommon sense of what could be unfolding, and I will find fertile ground for putting my ideas out there."

    Example 2: "I believe we are all the same" touches a deeper place when reshaped as "I believe every person has the same inherent value in Life, even as I recognize we have been shaped by different histories."

Experience gives us this depth. Don't let the self-judgment that you are not living up to your ideals hold you back. Consider these ideals as guideposts you can use to assess where you are in relation to where life has taken you—and how you will make choices from there.

If wounding messages from earlier times are too strong, slow down your reading and get that extra help to stand back and get perspective.

Progressively, you will begin to see how you would be behaving and feeling if you lived congruently with your chosen values and beliefs. You might even see immediate actions to take to start experiencing the inner peace that congruence brings.

    Example 1: If I value liberty and equality, I may need to re-examine how I treat those who are different from me. I will want to get to the truth about what I'm doing, not about what the other is or should be doing. I will feel hope.

    Example 2: If I believe in the sanctity of human life, I must live in ways that don't resort to addiction or violence to pacify fear. Fear will abate as I grow confident in and mobilize my own unique gifts.

*This is one way to work the personal leadership process: Using the entry points of values and beliefs, discerning how to bring behaviour into line with those values and beliefs, and then noticing what shifts in our emotions.*

*What beliefs is life experience causing me to re-evaluate?*
*What new ones am I willing to lead with?*

## Tune in with your emotions and get to the root of where they are coming from

- Ask yourself: What am I feeling? Where is this truly coming from? Then create an inner conversation with the emotion that responds affirmatively and constructively: What do you need? Will you let me find a better way to meet your need and take the lead?

Open a conversation between source, the emotion, and the wise witness who sees the need to lead from a different place: "I see you and am holding you both while we figure this out."

If the emotion is grief (old or recent), ask, "What are the values and beliefs I can bring to bear in expressing my experience of loss"? If you believe in life after death, you may hold onto the hope of eternity in heaven. If you value self-expression and believe in everyone's right to self-determine, you might create a personal piece of art to symbolize your relationship with what you've lost.

> Example 1: I have a friend who lost her daughter to carbon monoxide poisoning. The loss triggered in her a voice that had been silenced. She has painted some very beautiful pieces of her daughter.

> Example 2: Sitting at a family gathering recently, the woman beside me told me she must let go of being the mom whom her boys depend on to steer their lives. She took them to the beach this summer—both to help her self let go and to teach them about the natural timing of letting go of her, of finding their own inner compass.

Shame touches such a primal place in us that it can feel too tender to face and give words to. Expressing our desire for affection and human warmth, for sexual touch, should be natural. But we may have received mixed messages about being vulnerable, making desire uncomfortable. If the desire has become closeted (sexually, relationally, socially, religiously), it can go underground; shame and desire end up fighting each other.

While it is important to discern our distinct desires and find ways to express them respectfully, we can at least give them space in us so we can begin to embody what gives us joy—celebrating rites of passage, dancing to the sounds of tribal beats and rhythms, opening to orgasmic movements in our bodies. These feelings are congruent with values of tradition, aliveness, and relationship.

Emotions like anger and hatred are also difficult to hold and respond to. We can remain victims of them in the hope that the one who "caused" our anger and hate will heal us by doing the right thing. It can feel intimidating, deeply disturbing and disruptive, to sit with these emotions and get at their roots.

*The challenge in using emotion as an entry point into the personal leadership process is to take ownership of feelings that may have been triggered by others, but are really saying something about where we are on a personal level.*

Example 1: We often feel anger when we are invaded or seemingly denigrated by something or someone we don't know how to respond to. The Buddhist practice of mindfulness might ask us to take note of where we will draw the boundaries of our existence. Have we not drawn them at all but let something or someone deplete us? While our rage may serve to temporarily preserve our sense of power and space, it is ineffective over time.

Example 2: Hating and building walls against those we perceive as taking what we worked hard for is a complex and often divisive dilemma in immigration policy. Is our fear that there will not be enough left for us or that newcomers will make a mockery of our generosity?

When we allow our boundaries to metastasize and become brittle, we react out of a sense of survival. We don't take the time to stand back, breathe, and discern what the true intent of a person or situation might be. Only then can we know what balance of action needs to be taken.

Staying stuck in blame, shame, anger, or hatred is almost always a sign that we are not growing as we wish—as we demand others do. To admit that we are stuck is to do the inner work that frees us from the holes we've existed in.

Similarly, when we see someone else struggling to act in congruence with what they value and believe, we might ask them to take notice of what is happening for them. A value of respect demands that we give that person space to discern what is often more complicated than what we perceive from the outside.

What emotions have I not been facing, allowing them to block my growth? What are they inviting me to take ownership of now?

# Step back and take conscious note of how you are acting

When we are in survival mode, we are often not conscious of our behaviour. We don't yet see, or we are not ready to risk, what needs to be changed.

- Become aware of and take ownership of how you are acting in a situation, allowing any discomfort to transform something so deep in you that you are never again the same.

Example 1: Someone gives feedback, and all we hear is criticism, no matter how behaviour-based their observations are. We argue that we are not doing what they say we are doing. We project onto another the responsibility we wish we knew how to take. If we could really see what harm our actions inflict onto those we love, onto the causes we hope to influence, the exposure would move us so profoundly that we would develop whole new ways of being. We will put aside beliefs that make us fear risk and put out front what encourages us to grow.

Example 2: As parents, we want our children to grow in confidence and find their own sense of purpose. When those children inevitably meet the realities of human limitation (their own, ours, and others'), we need to stand back and reassess if our support is helping or hindering our child's need to learn what life is teaching. This is especially challenging when resources are few and there is little energy to re-examine what valuing self-determination will look like in our particular situation.

When we don't act in congruence with what we value and believe, a cycle of shame and defensiveness not only permeates our inner life—it is projected onto the relationships and cultures we exist in. This creates a toxicity that grows in direct proportion to our unwillingness to regroup and figure out what is truthfully driving our behaviour.

We can become so fixated on behaviour (our own or another's) that it becomes the issue of the day. Any deeper sense of what drives the now disordered behaviour stays buried in the psyches and souls of our lives, families, cultures, and nations.

*Using this entry point—uncovering what is driving*
*our personal and collective behaviour—is a*
*(potentially historic) opportunity to take*
*hold of what fundamentally needs*
*realignment.*

What behaviours of my own am I willing
to change, trusting this will strengthen
rather than threaten my confidence?

# Influencing the Larger Dilemmas of Life

The creative and evolutionary nature of this developmental process comes from the growing ability to move among our chosen values, beliefs, emotions, and behaviour. Any life experience can serve as an entry point for realigning what we discern to be true and how we choose to lead forward.

This progressive discernment of congruence is where the personal leadership process keeps our sense of call vibrant and responsive to the moments and contexts we exist in. Our inner and outer lives are woven and threaded in such a way that we are able to respond to the changing personal and social circumstances of our lives.

The dilemmas we personally and globally face are increasingly complex. How we reorganize to sustain meaning in that complexity will make our responses intelligent and capable of shaping a positive direction.

*Am I ready to let go (of assumptions, limiting emotions, defensive behaviours) if it means I could renew my sense of Life, have healthier relationships, be active in meaningful work?*

*Kate*

More than once Kate had to hear and accept truths that meant making deep change. She had to recognize when her ability to shape things around her was limited by forces she neither valued nor believed in.

By stepping back from the noise and letting Life hold her, she is creating (personal and cultural) spaces where dilemmas can be faced honestly, and where congruence can return.

Kate's way of taking hold of what she knew enabled her to move from a place of orchestrating what Life could be—for others, for a culture—to a place where she could choose to stand back or work with what was there. She could help others see there was so much more to life; she could see her own need to re-member to this purpose.

**Hearing the messages from her body**

I had learned over time to pay attention to Life's guidance. But, over the last three years, when the messages got louder and more persistent, I just didn't feel I had the energy to take on what was apparent—a big change. I was having physical symptoms of dread and sleeplessness. I had ignored these signs once before, almost at my peril. I tried many ways to keep going—rationalizing, avoiding, coming at it from different angles—but eventually it became crystal clear that I needed to let go of some things and stop bullshitting myself. It has taken some time to quiet myself so I could hear and understand what I needed to do.

**Sensing deeper truth**

**Life review; a sense of call and purpose**

I look back and see that my passion for *helping others understand there is so much more to life—more happening than just the event in front of them*—has always been there. I was the child with 101 questions; I had intense curiosity about life and how things worked! I was also someone who had a powerful sense of right and wrong, and a great need to take charge and not be told who I could be.

**Awareness of a value**

Significant people in my life have influenced these parts of my character. My mother was a caring but wounded woman. I have a clear picture even now of her standing and being unhappy in the kitchen, and me, seeing that there's trouble, gathering up my younger brother and sister to keep them out of the way. It was very hard as a kid, but I've come to terms with it now— she was an unhappy person—though my sensitivity to others remains.

My Gran fiercely lived out the Swedish motto *yentil yonum*, "the nail that stands up gets hammered down." In my Gran's world anything you did that made you stand out was problematic. Growing up, she was a big part of our lives, so it was "be quiet," "behave"! I can remember standing up to her on occasion, usually with a resulting slap! It didn't stop me; I felt what she was doing was wrong.

My father taught me one of my most valuable lessons about life. I was seven or eight. I came home in tears one day because I had been bullied again. I remember my dad saying, "It's time you learned to fight back. I'll show you how to defend yourself." The next time I got picked on, I just hauled off and smacked the lead bully, and that was the end of that! My dad taught me that sometimes you have to stand up for something.

**Early ways of
acting on her
values and beliefs**

I see how, over the years in my work, whether with patients or staff in an institution, this role of helping those who have struggled, who haven't had a voice, has landed back in my lap over and over again. I probably took on the roles, but I also saw they needed to be taken. In my nursing career, I was seen as someone who would stand up and say what others were afraid to say. In one hospital where nurses were being treated abysmally, as president of the union local, I rallied colleagues to start documenting overtime. This included confronting a CEO who had little respect for women or issues within the nursing ranks.

Later, when I began working in occupational health, I again took on this role of voicing the uncomfortable when a supervisor kept inappropriately brushing against and touching me and another nurse. Remember now that this was at a time when women had less power and voice in the workplace.

Another time, a colleague and I discovered that the head of Labour Relations was going into our confidential files; we went to speak with the plant president. He didn't see anything wrong with what was done. I did. I decided this information needed to be elevated and wrote the corporate CEO and the OCEW union president. Not surprisingly, I got walked off the job! Oh, I was devastated—an idealist young nurse—I thought I'd never find work in my field again.

**A situational
catalyst;
expanding her
understanding of
how to act on her
values and beliefs**

I did, however, go back into occupational health and that gave me the opportunity to meet a man who was to expand my world. Up to this point, I had the feisty part down pat, but he would sit me down and get me to take different angles on an issue, make it bigger. He was the head of Human Resources, a busy man, but he afforded me a huge amount of time to question: What else is going on here?

I was twenty-nine, then thirty years old, and beginning to stretch my awareness to larger organizational issues. I learned that, instead of immediately moving into action, there was value in standing back and asking questions, taking the time to talk to folks and walk around an issue, debate it, come at it from a number of angles. This man fed my curiosity and helped me expand the focus of that curiosity. He gave me a larger view of myself beyond nursing.

I realized that a constant for me had always been knowing that people had to tell their stories. Later, in establishing an employee assistance program, much of my work was offering time and space for people to come and just talk, tell me what was happening in their department, listening with them for what could be done. Eventually, I moved into an employee advocate position with a banking organization. There, over 10 years, my purpose was to enable people to see themselves and their situations in different ways, to take action.

My position was the brainchild of the company president, who was an incredibly forward thinking man. Sad to say that when the next president came in, although he was a kind and deeply experienced man in banking, he didn't understand people very well. We moved away from a focus on what was right to what was expedient.

Ultimately, that affected my role because people were reluctant to speak out. I started to see and feel a lot of toxicity building up as people had nowhere to put their frustrations—or even understand them! I could advise and listen, though more and more in a limited way. The larger issues were not addressed.

**Sensing her body speak; knowing an inner truth**

I began to feel diminished in my role. I saw things, but began to back away from what could be done. There was little fire in my belly to fight the system. I felt myself contract inside, not wanting to pick up the phone because I knew I might have to say, "The options are few here in your circumstance." That was the hardest part—not being able to bring voice to the truth—at least as I saw it.

I kept trying to practice what I had been taught, to back up and look at situations from different perspectives.

I rationalized and I avoided but, over time, began to feel I was prostituting myself. People weren't being listened to in any real way. My boss commented that I really only dealt "with the bottom of the barrel" anyway. That shook me, and I realized I had to leave. Though there were times I felt I had failed, I began to make peace with the realization that my time in the organization was done.

I have been angry at times, but see now that perhaps I had been most angry at my self. "My god, Kate, you see this happen to other people"! When it's time for a change and you don't pay attention, the noise in your life gets louder.

**Holding her self
and working to
come back into
congruence;
building
new inner
conversations
that felt alive
and that opened
possibilities**

I started dialoging with my body, saying, "I hear you . . . here's what I'm going to do." The tension inside eased the more I acted on my promise to lead my life in a way that made sense to me. Amazing things began to happen. For the first time in my marriage, my husband is earning the money, and I get to be the one moving in new directions! He had always been restless when it came to work; he's moved around a lot.

This had been my excuse for staying in situations too long. The truth is I accepted that role because I got to be the boss lady! This did cause difficulties at one point—we almost divorced. It was coming to a place of not blaming each other, stepping up to what we each contributed to our situation, and a healthy dose of daily genuine appreciation that turned things around.

It was huge for me to step away from being the CEO of the universe, to get out of my head and trust the wisdom of my body. It's not that my body hadn't spoken to me before. Twelve years ago, I had cancer. I didn't choose cancer, but it did get my attention, and I did make some changes. But it is the wisdom I am growing now at fifty-four that enables me to accept that though my boss lady made brave attempts to help people be who they could be, it doesn't need to happen in a particular way. I don't have to push myself so hard anymore. I simply have to be willing to be patient and allow things to be revealed to me. When we come to our work each day, we can be the creative force that moves through us—I call it Spirit.

**Life review:
maturing of her
call; shifting
attachment to a
spiritual source**

**Sustaining congruence between her values, beliefs and actions, noticing the shift in emotion; returning to "there is so much more to life!"**

I am currently building my own company where I endeavour to help people realize potential, channeling that purpose through my roles as coach and facilitator of dialogue in workplaces. I only take on assignments where I sense there is a will to move. I see that when people come together and bring their best thinking into open space, there is a wonderful state of emergence where important things get talked about in a productive way—and it just feels so good! There is a palpable shift in how the culture begins to redefine what the work is really about, what their success indicators will be.

# Being with Each Other in a Way that Challenges and Opens a Greater Sense of Truth

*Something inside begins to move and shift;*
*we open and move together.*

You feel more confident, stronger, less reactive, and more able to see what is truly in front of you. You aren't as bothered by things and people that once unnerved you; you might even feel compassion toward their situation. You understand more about their motivations than your fear had previously allowed you to. The differences you had with others and the prejudices you defended are now exposed; you begin seeing those hard lines as less necessary to your survival.

Each time I do my inner work and stand back, reassess, *then* respond, I know what it is to be free. In those moments, I see better what matters if a dynamic is to move forward. I know that I am okay and will be okay—whatever external circumstances bring.

It's not that I care less about what is around me. Rather, I'm able to care from a deeper place in my soul because I am not afraid to lose myself in something that, in the end, has no power to define me. A spiritual knowing inside liberates me. I understand that there will always be more to learn.

I begin to see that I need others in my life to learn with. Hopefully, they will be kindred spirits. In reality, I accept that those I walk with may agitate me deeply. They help me see and face even greater truths than those I could sense and open alone.

# New Understandings

These shifts in us—of congruence, confidence, strength, and clarity—suggest that we are ready to invite in and stay with the growing complexities of living in realities larger than our own. Others are seen, not as hindrances to where we aim to go, but companions and partners in Life.

Two insights will help us stay with these growing complexities:

1. Creation expresses itself in a myriad of ways where we are each a thread in the larger story, and

2. What we believe about the nature of others, and of what holds us jointly, will determine if and how we work with others to influence that story.

## Creation expresses itself in a myriad of ways

We get excited and energized about what is happening in our lives, thinking that what is being revealed to us is how everyone sees it. We can feel betrayed when others assert their right to their own discoveries.

The desire to be understood and have companions on our journey is healthy. The challenge is to:

- Be a companion to each other, gather around what is presenting for us both to learn.

The value and action required here is respect and responsibility. It is each of us saying, "*I am willing to participate in what is trying to grow here. I no longer wish to overload an already complicated situation.*"

Everything we have been working on up to now enables us to:

- Allow this space for new experiences—of connection and trust—to unfold.

We are held within what is beyond the human moment, freed to reorient to that moment. We are grasping less and listening more for what is trying to move in our encounter with one another.

Crushing fear may return, especially when change comes fast or the risk in opening is great. But we have core skills to work with now. We can stand back and deepen our practice with those skills—focus on what we are here to influence at this moment, pay attention to our bodies' signals and wisdom, clarify what is and is not ours to own, talk fear into its place.

We can trust that our inherent worth is not dependent on the outcome of this moment with another. There is more to see, more than our small selves have been willing to accept.

*Weaving my Story Into the Larger Story*

*When I recall a situation where I've had a powerful sense of the presence of another, how did I respond? What does this say I believe about what is beyond my own ability to control or create?*

# What we believe about the nature of others

We must have a second insight if we are going to have the capacity not only to stay with the complexity before us but also choose how to relate with others in it.

- What do I believe about the nature of others and what holds us jointly?

Martin Buber in his classic work, *I and Thou,* paints relationship as a mutual encounter of sacredness through which we "gaze toward the eternal you . . . perceive [the] breath of it"[8] in each other. He proposes that seeing another, not as means to our ends but as part of the very Life source that moves through us both, draws us into mutual relationship with sacred source. Margaret Wheatley expresses it as *bearing witness* with each other as we turn toward and allow the experience of the other to "enter our hearts."[9]

For this Life energy to be realized, each must be willing to:

- Risk and surrender all preconceptions of and attachments to the objectified form of the other.

A greater essence can then emerge and unleash its creativity in that third space.

In the embrace of this third and sacred Life presence, love and meaning deepen; we come to see clearer the pulse of Life wanting to move and be "born"[10] through the moment we share. It is a moment of re-membering into our "genuine original unity."[11] It is a moment of hope.

The lines that define us are not blurred; we are uniquely held in this third embrace. What unifies us is preserved; we sense its presence.

*In seeing one another, we see our selves.*
*We feel accountable to something greater than fear.*

When I place between me and "other" what I think is that third value/ethic/creative energy we are both trying to experience, what do I sense changing, deepening?

# Skills

Two skills can strengthen our resolve and grow our trust, enabling us to remain open and attentive to what is trying to emerge through an encounter with another. The purpose here is to *expand our sense of what connects us* to others, and what it is that deepens that bond.

We grow beyond our fearful need to limit what relationship can be as we:

1. Use imagery that moves us beyond divisiveness, and

2. Sustain connection through the third presence.

## Use imagery that moves us beyond divisiveness

Images offer a visceral way to begin exploring the possibility of sacred connection. We tend to limit our attentions to Life in singular form (my needs, your way, the leader's responsibility, your opinion, my culture, the government's responsibility—even God's way). Opening to larger truth requires expanding the boundaries of our existence in a way that doesn't weaken our personal experience. Rather, we are energized in realizing we are a necessary part of that greater whole.

- Sit back and make room for this sense of the whole of Life to come to you, then picture and create what you sense. (A place to bring in your art supplies or journal).

Popular images of what connects us include bridges, webs, a common Life pulse, shared purpose and directionality (hope, gathering to realize a mission). If you are looking for inspiration, visit museums and art shows, and browse the Internet for symbols and visuals that resonate, stirring something deep inside you. The world is full of expressive ideas about what most simply holds and draws us together—despite, and even because of, our growing complexities. You might feel drawn to create your own personal image.

- Make your image relevant by holding it in real time. As you sit and listen to another, make no anxious interruptions or superficial reassurances, simply remain present and hold the image.

Even if the image is fleeting, even if holding it doesn't resolve a dilemma, being willing to hold the image over time keeps the space open for something to come through later. It may simply be letting the image be of that holding space "between the way things are and the way we know they might be . . . a space that never will be closed."[12]

I personally know the depth of trust in Life this patient waiting demands. I am there now. I notice my parents aging and see us all trying to let this transition flow gracefully into the story of what our family will become. I left Zimbabwe eight months ago with no obvious resolution on particular issues, but with the image of the day we sat around a circle of stones—sometimes leaning into, other times sitting back from the circle.

## Sustain connection through the third presence

Sometimes holding a unifying image is not enough to sustain the often competing and human dynamics in a relationship. Efforts to stay personally aligned in our vision of the whole rubs up against how the other envisions relationship. We may have different perspectives, use different language, in how we work with that whole. And there is always the noise and distraction that unhealed wounds (broken trusts from "authority" figures; personal, cultural, or racial abuses) project into any relational space.

To preserve a sense of wholeness while making room for those new perspectives to shape how we approach our human complexities requires a second skill: sustaining connection through the wisdom and witness of the third presence. This can simply be the presence of truth itself. We all search for truth; the challenge is accepting that *no one* can claim superior ownership of it.

It may be an image that has particular meaning in a relationship. My husband and I return to an image of the surf each anniversary, to notice the personal movements we are (or need to be) making to deepen our bond. The surf is our witness; it has something to reveal to us each year as we take the time and space to sense the wisdoms in its rhythm.

Sometimes the presence exists in that space *amidst* us, drawing us around it. Other times we stand *in it* for the larger view it offers on what may have become so complicated that we can no longer see what is trying to come through.

By making room for or standing in the third space, we gain a new lens. We see more clearly the truth of what *is* happening in our situations. The work is to:

- Reposition your small selves (help them stand back and become open to learn) so you can expand and deepen what you both come to understand. (This is not an easy process. You may want to work with a therapist or wise friend to help you gain the space and do the work).

- Experiment with images of a third presence that energizes, invites, and draws you both. Putting words to the image can expand the essential meaning you attach to it—trust, love, openness, even a poem. On the image my husband and I revisit, a verse speaks to the intimacy of walking together, talking, listening, sharing fears and hopes.

Make these visuals energies that make you want to explore and move toward them. Shared commitment to a sense of flow keeps the energies between us moving.

*From the stance of witness, there is no assumption*
*of something needing to be fixed, only a*
*sense of curiosity and making room to see together*
*what is trying to grow through the vessel of us.*

There is also no need for each one to be at the same place of readiness. The space can be held in the physical, even spiritual, absence of the other, though time must bring both to the space if something greater than one is to be matured. Discerning how much of our selves we keep invested in holding that space requires wisdom, or too much time will pass and too much of our energy will be drained by lack of creative growth. Connection is our original and natural state. We retain both the right and responsibility to:

- Determine which connections continue to feel alive and challenge you to grow.

The art of joining our lives around collective energies can be fraught with so many fears and obstacles that we despair. The will to stay in a process is evidence of our belief in that process. We trust that even in the absence of obvious change, something new is trying to take form.

How will I do my part to stay open to what my relationships challenge me to see—even when I feel afraid?

# Brad and Jan

Brad and Jan came to see how old personal wounds tainted what they believed to be the motives of each other. By opening up to deeper personal truths and holding the images of their wounded selves in a different way, they gained the space of witness. This allowed them to appreciate the different ways they orient to Life and how they can create something that is unique to them.

The dialogue form illustrates the skills this couple used, including the young values and needs they are building their deeper sense of relationship upon. Their story begins in the present, loops back into their histories, then returns to the present with new and deeper understanding.

The tender story of Brad and Jan speaks to the multiple pieces presenting in their marriage and work life. Touching on these varied aspects of their relational lives shows how interconnected our relationship history is. Movement in one will often touch some kind of movement in the other.

# Brad and Jan's Story

**Jan:** When we met in your law office, I saw you as handsome, bright, and sort of mysterious.

**Brad:** I was drawn to your beauty. You were soft, loving. Looking back now, I see that in a way I might have been hoping you could be a replacement for my mother, and you were a good moral person. You were a soft piece of light. There was goodness, destination, a place where I knew I wanted to go to complete myself.

**Wounds shaping his perspective of her**

**Jan:** There is a tradition of strong resilient women in my family—from my great-grandmother's pioneering spirit to my own mother's stoic life and death. What I saw growing up was that women held things together. I denied for a long time that I wanted someone to look after me. But because I didn't communicate that to you, things became confused. Years went by—I felt you let me down.

**Wounds shaping her perspective of him**

**Brad:** I was trying to connect with your vulnerable side but I found out you had trouble being with that part of yourself. I didn't understand that, and what I perceived was that you were just unwilling to be with me. I kept trying to connect by insisting we talk about our emotions. It didn't come, and what started happening was, because of old wounds from my adoption, it meant I wasn't worthy or didn't deserve it.

I became critical of you, implying in subtle ways that you were not able to share in the way I had with Bev [a previous relationship]. The more I tried to connect, the more desperate I felt about trying to make this marriage work. There was a sense that it just could not fail.

I was born to a woman who was not prepared to keep me, and I have carried a belief of not being welcome in the world, not being worthy or having a place, most of my life. This loss was the event that shaped more of my life than any other, it seems.

I have difficulty recalling memories from my childhood, but some stand out. I was raised in a Mennonite

**Old belief about his own nature; that belief shaping how he saw him self**

family where there was an emphasis on telling the truth. I remember an experience when my father was in university. I was about five or six years old, and my friends and I were helping him spread gravel around the garage. He gave us each a quarter to go to Al's corner store.

I bought some things and stole some more, and came back with probably a whole box worth of stuff. My dad asked me where I got it all. I said, well, with the money you gave me. He pointed out that I had more things than the money could have bought. So he walked me back to Al's corner store and stood behind me while I explained to the old proprietor what I had done. I've often reflected on how early in my life that happened and the embarrassment of having to confront Al. But there was a sense of things being made right.

**Shaping of a value: "truth" mattering**

Education was also a strong value given to me. When I had trouble learning how to read in Grade 1, at night I remember my parents would sit me down in front of a chalkboard and print words. I didn't get it, but I could feel how important it was to them that I learn these things. So I was shocked when in Grade 12, having become quite disillusioned with school and skipping 70 per cent of my classes but still maintaining good grades, my father said, "I think you're wasting your time there, and you should get a job." I was shocked that he wouldn't press me to get an education.

By that time, I was already buried into a pervasive feeling of aloneness. I'm thinking now as far back as five or six. My parents were living in the university area. I remember being in a wooden wagon with a little pillow inside for my knee, wagoning around in the neighborhood by myself, checking things out. That kid was looking for something.

**Early sense of third space: seeking connection—that wasn't there for either of them**

**Jan:** I remember feeling it was important for me to create a balance, that it was my role to read other people around me and have a calming effect, try to get rid of any negative emotions. Being the middle child between a rowdy brother and hyper sister, I was rewarded and appreciated for being able to settle things down.

But I also thought making others matter meant I was less important. I learned to stop my own feelings and

**Early belief about her self**

responses. I didn't learn how to process what I was feeling. I don't remember my mother being very emotional about anything. For a long time I thought of myself as lucky for having such an even-tempered mother.

**Brad:** Searching was my way of life for many years, always hungering for the truth of who I was. Last year, when you and I entered therapy, I had this epiphany, this incredible, almost physical outpouring of grief and loss, and pain—that felt as if coming from my experience when I was inside Lilly, and then being separated from her. I realized how long I had been carrying a sense that I wasn't welcome in the world. I've been afraid of loss throughout my whole life. I was driven by a mistrust of things as they appeared—the cynicism.

Powerful image of wounded self, of severed connection

The first place I remember feeling that I belonged was when I began playing guitar. I was fourteen or fifteen. I found a place where I was able to connect with my emotions and experience them by playing music. That gave me my young man's dream, which was to play in bar bands. My classmates were going off to university, and I played in the band—that's what I aspired to. This was a milestone for me in being able to express my feelings in public. The music helped me channel my grief so that I didn't end up like one of my present [criminal law] clients.

I loved the music but it didn't fill that empty place inside for long. There was a dark, depressed time. I remember feeling there was no ground, no direction. Wanting so much to find some truth, being so struck by the polarity of everything in life—everything seeming opposite, nothing absolute—having no feeling of purpose and lots of aloneness. That was my first deep depression.

I got through it by realizing I was in some kind of paralysis, that I needed to get myself out of it by first finding a purpose. So I made a deal with myself—if life makes no more sense at forty, I could end my life. Just take a step. I engaged more with people around me. I got a job in the electronics field, and that's where I met Bev, the first love of my life, a woman sixteen years older than me. It felt like she was the first person who saw, like me, some of the crazy, farcical elements of life. She left her husband; I went back into a band. This was one of the few places where I could still feel an exchange of energy, a dynamic that I was part of.

Visceral image of restrained self

**Jan:** As a teen, holding my self in showed up in a couple of ways. Eventually, I would have these outbursts to release bottled up emotion; I was promptly sent to my room. I think I was naturally sensitive, but asking for sensitivity seemed to get me nowhere. I just remember feeling, *Oh no, this is bad.*

At the same time, I felt a great desire to be with my family. I remember having a strong sense of security with them, that they were always there for me. I had other relationships and friends, though I don't remember going looking for them. They would call me to go out, but I was just happy to stay home.

When I started dating, I remember feeling quite torn. When I was with my friends, they were number one; when I was with my boyfriend, he was number one. Sometimes this meant I would completely walk away from someone; sometimes it meant an outburst. Either way, I turned my back on my feelings.

For example, when there was tension between Dave [a boyfriend] and my family, I moved to another province with him. I didn't face these two opposing forces in my life. I had known inside for a while that he wasn't right for me, and it got harder to make people happy. I just got to a place where I could no longer not act.

Listening to messages from her body

**Brad:** One day Bev got me into the car, drove me to the parking lot of the local law school, and said, "This is where I think you should go." I don't remember feeling drawn to law school. I had taken a commerce degree: I could be a professional after four years. But in my philosophy courses, I realized I was much more interested in reasoning with words than with numbers.

Law felt like an area of applied philosophy that would somehow directly affect people. Though I was initially intrigued by the whacked out stories in criminal cases, I began practicing in public utilities law. Eventually I found that it dried up my soul, and I began hating my job.

At one point I got to do an impaired charge trial, and I felt totally energized being at the courthouse. There was

Listening to messages from his body

a renewed sense of vitality in what law meant to me. My client was now a person and not a corporation.

I remember being afraid that criminal law would make me more skeptical than I already was, but I could *connect with the person's story and felt I was part of something, that I could help.* They were on the outside with their faces pressed against the glass, looking in—and part of me was standing there with them.

**Early sense of Life call, and a potent image: freeing the imprisoned self**

Just before writing the LSAT, and while leaving the relationship with Bev, I began searching for my birth mother. I remember spending afternoons in the public library with the directories, trying to locate my family and my mother. Nothing was working out.

About that time, I remember seeing a poster in a gym with a picture of something soft, a teddy perhaps, and there were the words: "I must be a somebody because God don't make no junk." I remember just feeling offended by the perception that adoptees were junk. This was a second time of deep depression.

My relationship of six years was ending. My future in terms of school was uncertain as I was not working. I was looking for my birth mother, and I wasn't getting anywhere. It seemed that all the measures I had used to define my self—student, employee, boyfriend—were gone and I was left with my self. It just felt empty.

I don't remember at that time having any sense of some great resolution, but I found a vague sense of something within me, of who I was, nothing more. I went out, wrote the LSAT, got a job, and started law school that autumn.

**Image of a divided heart**

**Jan:** You and I started a family so soon, and my feelings just got buried deeper and deeper. I had a baby to look after, a husband to look after, and I made those priorities. I hadn't planned this first pregnancy and was only twenty-one. But it was exciting too because there you were, ready to marry me and make everything okay. I liked that.

At first, it was exactly what I wanted. I was a busy parent, but I tried to get in touch with myself too. I was just going through the motions though—a friend would drag me to a class, or Deb and I would go painting. It just brushed the surface. You craved a deeper emotional connection with me, and I wasn't even in touch with my own feelings. When you didn't get that kind of intimacy from me, you pulled away, into yourself and your work.

I was left alone with kids, caring for this, making sure that happened, being just like the other women in my family. Women didn't complain, didn't talk about emotions, so I found myself in a situation where I was being exactly what I thought I would grow up to be. But it didn't really satisfy me. It didn't put me in a place to get in touch with my self, or to be vulnerable—it did the opposite. I got more resentful and probably less willing to give you what you wanted from me. I don't know who started to change first, but I got to a point where even though I knew I could continue, I also knew it wasn't really me.

Her own limitations prompting inner attachment

**Brad:** What I did for a long time was sit in the corner, but at the same time blaming and beating myself up for running away, for not being good enough. You might remember this was when—right in the middle of my first murder trial, the biggest roller-coaster ride I've ever been on—I got that call from my birth mother. I remember sitting in the kitchen, waiting for her call. It was the first time I allowed myself to recognize how important it was. I had had my name on the registry since I was eighteen, and she had never called before, but now I allowed myself to feel how much it mattered. Initially, I had a lot of scenarios of how it would go, but in the end, it didn't matter as much as I thought it would. I listened to her story, but my loneliness, the hole inside my self, stayed.

Sensing the need for a greater source of attachment

One night, sitting in my car in the dark, I saw this little boy yelling up at me, "I haven't done anything wrong now stop beating me up you fucker"! This was my epiphany, and I was finally able to find my little boy self, to hold him and stop beating him up. I learned that what I was so desperately trying to get from you, Jan, was inside me. When I first started to realize I was really trying to find the missing piece of myself, I could start seeing you for who you were versus who I was perceiving or wanting you to be.

Raw image of violated self; holding wounded self

A new belief about who she is

Once I was able to hold my self and feel love from my Creator, I felt compelled to share that with you. That emptiness I felt all my life is being filled now and I feel free. I see that I am no more or less entitled than anyone else in this world—that we're all the same in some ways, just on personal journeys.

Third space
becoming
clearer: Both
are beginning
to witness the
journey of their
lost selves, and
their deep and
mutual desire
for connection

**Jan:** I see that my sensitivity had turned into something it wasn't meant to be. I got lost in there. I lost being able to recognize my own feelings. This showed up in our marriage.

I was hoping that what I wanted would come in the form of another person—someone to look after me, be a voice for me. If I did what others wanted, I thought, I would be taken care of in return. Even when my mother died—I was about twenty-six—I still deflected the loss and made it about my dad. I still feel that pain of losing her and then needing someone to look after me. I was very much like my mom, putting other people first.

I appreciate your reflectiveness now—and the goodness that comes from it. It's new to me. It takes a certain amount of courage and self-confidence to share one's self; I am working on this. That you are cutting me some slack has given me the freedom to get things out without worrying whether I will offend or hurt you, or make a bad impression. Sharing my insecurities and vulnerabilities feels right now. You are listening to me, and I've not sent you running yet! I can see the flow back and forth between us because I am expressing more and more.

Opening and
holding her
vulnerable self

Aligning new
beliefs with new
behaviour

**Brad:** I was in my head a lot. I feel that exchange of deeper energy now, and I'm learning to connect with you and with others, with the crowd, the world. Part of the reason I felt I didn't belong was because there was another whole level of conversation going on that I wasn't aware of. Something is happening inside, something that makes me question how I am in many aspects of my life.

I notice that I am more sensitive to Ben, the son whose paternity I had questioned. I convinced myself it didn't matter because of the love I had always felt from my adoptive parents. All my life I had rejected my own inner child, who was given away. Perhaps I unconsciously rejected Ben by avoiding him; he reminded me of myself.

In my work, you know how I talk about whether what I'm doing is the best way to help. Sometimes in my cynical moods I tell people that what I do for a living is help people not become accountable for their actions. I've been uncomfortable with that for a long time. But I also keep thinking about this kid that I helped who had a terrible methamphetamine habit and he committed terrible acts of violence. He went to jail for quite a while.

I met him a couple of years later at a golf course, and he thanked me for changing his life. It felt like I did very little, but the more I've thought about it, the more I realize that what I did was spend time sitting with him and his pain in a small cubicle at the Remand Centre.

**Jan:** I participate in my relationships now. I think I can still be a peacemaker without sacrificing myself so much. I have a strong sense of family still. Studying interior design and working in my father's business as a home designer is drawing me back to me; it's a way to *express and create.* Earlier, I thought about designing but talked myself out of it for lack of confidence. I see how important it is to teach my children to be emotionally honest with themselves and in their relationships. I take comfort knowing I get the chance to express myself in ways women before me were not able to.

**Brad:** I am carving out a way now to *practice justice that can restore—not just my soul—but hopefully my client's as well.*

There is a gentler way to belong, forgive and be forgiven. I'm finding it, going solo in my practice—on the outside but no longer just looking in.

Third space:
Both drawing
around their
desire for deeper
connections,
seeing what gets
created when they
let wounds and
perceptions go

Re-membering
to an early call
to create

Re-visiting
and discerning
his Life call

COLLEEN MAC DOUGALL

# Keeping Alive our Deepest Truth as We Walk its Path

*There comes a contentment that transcends situational happiness, a wisdom that has been grown through time.*

It is a quiet powerfulness that no longer needs to falsely assert itself. We feel at peace, softened, whole. We know where we "belong."

These are times in the journey that are to be revered and cherished as markers in our transformation. The word transformation captures the revelatory experience of what the waves of Life continue to wash into our being, deeply changing how we see Life with us. We are energized; we feel restored.

It is here that I believe the meaning of our journey, and our call, takes on the deepest significance. The focus now shifts even more to what is beyond the power of the personality, to creating new relational experiences that free us to be *in* Life's presence without having to fear it.

We feel less and less need to objectify the other as we become progressively able to see deeper truths unfold before our very eyes, usually quite rapidly now. We invest less in getting issues "right" or solved. We become clearer about what the matters before us truly are—and how uncertain the journey to any truth about those matters can be.

*We release our assumptions and absolutions of truth, and remain open to the "eternal conversation"[13] that truth is.*

# New Understandings

Coming to this softened powerfulness is a strange mix of being humbled and strengthened. The sense is not that we are free of fear, but that we have become capacitated in letting fear open us. We see, and even welcome, the need to take hold of our part in helping to evolve the Life of the whole.

It is ever more apparent to us that:

1. There is an evolutionary movement between our human existence and the creative purpose of Life with us, preparing us for the tasks ahead; and

2. That we remain open to how the call to lead will reveal itself.

## Evolutionary movement between human existence and Life purpose

One way we keep our call real, vibrant, and responsive to the context and times in which we live is to:

- Keep breathing with how Life itself is moving.

There is awareness and acceptance now that we are not master of the waves—they will keep moving. But as we stand and watch them, we know how essential it is that we move with them.

We need not fear losing our selves in their unending movement; we might more fear missing the invitations along the way that help us claim our place in them. Even so, when an opportunity passes by, we trust another time will come.

> *We are ready for what the next wave will bring.*
> *We sense a deep harmony with those waves—they,*
> *and our inner movements, seem as one.*
> *We allow them to touch us.*

We intentionally seek out places where we can reconnect with their rhythm. We re-member our nature as we sense our lives, including what we are ready to release, blending into the expansiveness of the sea.

*Returning to my Innocent Sense of Call*
When I revisit my earliest memories of what energized me and formed in me a sense of purpose: Where have I lived congruently with that? Where have I become confused, fearing I had lost my way?

## Remaining open to how the call to lead will reveal itself

Deepening how we come to understand the call to full Life demands this second willingness, to:

- Remain open to the evolving nature and intent of our call to lead.

I am reminded of how, even during the process of writing this book, my sense of what I knew eight years ago—that I needed to bring my care outside the boundaries of my office—has deepened and been cultivated. I wrote the first edition of this book in my first year out of practice; I wrote *Restoring our World Soul* in between.

> *The space has given me experience and time to see deeper*
> *into what it means to care about and support*
> *leadership within contexts with their own*
> *value systems and sense of what matters.*

Confronted in my western notions—of what inactivity must mean, what should just be overcome, and to what end social inequities can be fought—I am returned. I am asked to:

- Re-member, again and again, keep out front the heart and soul of who I am and why I am here at this moment.

Doing the personal work that helps me lead from a place that is as true as I can discern at any one time, is deeply congruent with my value of creative justice.

It was a poignant moment when, at the end of my time with a Canadian leader recently, I heard myself say, "I remember why I wrote *A Very Personal Leadership*." Preparing for retreats and helping create a number of learning encounters, I've read this book many times—and over time. Each time, my own words take up deeper residence in me.

I re-member why I began this work. Witnessing a world and a generation of youth search for meaning in chaos, young therapists and even experienced educators bravely step out, using their distinct lens to impact the here and now of global dilemmas, I feel Life move in me and nod, *yes*.

I see my self trying to stay open to where this way of leading with Life will take me. T.S. Eliot's message gives me comfort: that our purpose at any one time is "beyond the end [we] figured . . . and is altered in the fulfillment."[14]

*What signals am I getting now that some deeper call is trying to be expressed through my life?*

# Skills

For each of us, there is a fierce tenacity within spurring us to open and stay connected to what is meaningful and purposeful when what we face seems like too much. We search for ways to keep our call alive, to let it evolve—because the world we live in is evolving.

This *deepening engagement between what we value and believe, and what our evolving world demands* is activated as we:

1. Intentionally seek out and explore new connections, and

2. Revisit and discern what our Life call asks of us now.

## Seek out and explore new connections

Few of us are willing to stay on a demanding course without support. We want to know we are not alone, that we are not crazy to see things the way we do. We yearn to be encouraged to act on what we hear inside ourselves.

Such support isn't always nearby. Eight summers ago, when visiting the homes of famous artisans, I first felt the deep rush of kindred spirits with my writing. Their stories often included that same sense of being on the outside I had always felt was true for me. Sometimes support comes from unexpected sources.

- Travel to new places, expose your self to new theologies and paradigms, seek and receive the feedback of others, reread journal entries and wise and holy texts for the meaning they now reveal—these are just a few concrete ways we remain seekers of our own destiny. And even as we seek it, our understanding of what destiny is evolves.

## Revisit and discern our Life call

A second and final skill that can help us actively deepen our call to affect Life is akin to the life review, but it integrates now all we've experienced and learned through our developmental choices along the way (i.e., the way of the river).

- Take the space and go back to re-member both your innocent sense of call, and the chosen values and beliefs that fit with that call. See how what holds meaning and significance for your life has been reshaped, matured, through the experiences and turning points in between.

Every time we listen to, grow in, and act on how we are being asked to lead now, we deepen our capacity to influence those powerful purposes we once felt innocently drawn to.

I still care about everything that wants to live. My young assumptions—that I must care about all that needed care, that I knew best what care would look like in another's life and context—have been challenged. Expectations about what responses are appropriate from these others, even what is necessary if we are all to help move a different world forward, are still being peeled back. I continue to see clearer what *it is* that I care about.

Caring is more than an act. It is an embodiment of what lives in me and calls me to purpose.

*What new connections am I making, will I make, to keep my Life work alive, expansive, and responsive to the world I live in now?*

# Patrick

He opened. He listened. He acted on what he heard. This—his will to let his sense of call evolve in the midst of what Life brought—kept his spirit alive and connected to what was beyond him and his moment here in time.

Patrick tells his story of returning to what he sensed call him early in life—to be part of something bigger—with a deepening sense of what that means. The meager religious, abusive, and restorative experiences he lived, and the global connections he made that opened ways to keep his sense of call responsive, taught him how to bring a peaceful end to his human life.

# *Patrick's Story*

I was the young lad who sought out safe places—in my room, cleaning the church with my father, setting out mass and serving the priest underneath my cassock and surplice (altar boy's garments). I was naturally introspective, though it was probably my mother's commitment to Catholicism and our family's need for money that landed me my job with the church.

**Early sense of a call**

I liked it well enough—played out the whole priest thing in my room—to the point where my mother would proudly announce to everyone that her boy was going to be a priest! This is one of my earliest memories of sensing I was to play a religious role in my life. My mother, all 300 pounds of her, imprinted the idea, but I also felt some affinity with it. It was no more than a boy's innocent sense that he wanted to *be part of something bigger than himself,* and God seemed like a good place to start.

I was a different kid, tall and thin as a rake, with (to this day) very different views on how life worked. Our family was poor; we were the kids who wore what social services and the local charities gave out.

Yet, I was the first in Grade 11 to get my own car. I still remember it—an old red bug—I earned every dollar to pay for it! I was the guy who didn't question what I was told at home, but I also accepted little about what others seemed to think was true. At that age, I didn't know anyone who particularly thought like I did and certainly no one who took an interest in what I thought . . . until I gravitated toward the presbytery.

There was a priest who took me under his wing, and we would spend endless hours together. It was mostly him who talked—I was just looking for a place to connect with something, *somebody* to tell me I fit *somewhere.* I caught onto deep ideas quickly and felt he appreciated my company. He was sort of a mystery to me, but I liked this.

It is very hard for me to explain this to others, how drawn I became to him, the liturgy, the bigness and old power of his world—and how small I began to feel at the same time. Even now, forty-four years later, I remember how right it felt to be with him in his world, and how afraid I was too. I had been taught that the priest was next to God, so it must be okay, no? The confusion started.

I remember the first time—I was eleven years old—the priest invited me into his private room. Probably to a lad who naturally sought private places, this would have intrigued me. The priest gradually told me more about his childhood, how different he felt, how he knew early on that he wanted to serve God. It was like talking to a friend—this one *was* interested in me.

It didn't go further for quite a while, but one day, after about half a year, he put his hand on my back, tender-like. I remember my body tensing, but I didn't say a word. I guess he thought that gave him permission and the touching became more frequent, lower on my body. Again, I said nothing, just froze. I felt so confused, and what would I tell about anyway? I was the one going to his house! For three years the touching continued, and he did violate me in ways I find hard to admit even to myself. The shame went very deep.

Then one day—I was about fourteen—it just stopped. I stopped going to the parish house; he stopped talking to me. More confusion. The next four years I stumbled around. I never got into alcohol. Girls weren't attractive except as friends. I remember my mother harping about when I was going to think about training as a priest, that the parish was willing to talk to me and maybe help me. I continued to play my trombone and read a lot—some were books the priest had given me.

I did eventually end up in the priesthood—and I kept my secret. In those years, no one wanted to know anyway. I was assigned a parish that was far away from where I grew up (and where the priest who had abused me still served). I was good at my new role, and I gained a reputation for being good with the youth. All went along well until I learned one day that a charge was being laid against the priest who had been my "friend."

I was stunned, frozen—like I was eleven years old again. I had pushed this aside for a long time. Who could I confess to when I had in some confused way allowed it to happen? Sexual abuse by priests was still something the church did not acknowledge, certainly not publicly. I was that church!

I listened intently over the next several months to the details of the charge, watched the Church's response—and felt sicker every day. I knew, I knew. At the end of this, I went to see my old priest friend and told him that I would keep the secret if he came forward to somehow help this other young boy he had violated. It didn't happen, and I lost something there, perhaps my faith in human beings.

**Feeling betrayed by others; keeping his behaviour aligned with his values and beliefs**

I took a sabbatical and went to serve in a parish in South America. I have some Spanish blood in me, and I fit in; I almost found a new sense of calling there. The poverty and the desperation—they were familiar to me. I probably wouldn't have ended up there if not for the scandal back in Canada, but I sensed something change in me. Down there, liturgy was more immediate. People were more trusting in a simple kind of way. Politics were raw, not tight-lipped. It touched my heart—ripped it open actually.

**Seeking renewed connections, even as they were loosely chosen**

**A situational catalyst**

Again, it was the young people who drew me to them. You know how they say that history gives us another chance? Maybe it did. A new family in my parish had a six-year-old boy, Samuel. He would follow me around, tug at my pockets. He couldn't speak a word of English. Soon there were a few boys. Then a group of boys.

I was getting nervous because, remember, I was still holding my secret, and I knew about the fire spreading in North America that was making all priests nervous. I served in South America for another five years. We built a small but tight-knit group of youth, doing lessons together but never in my private quarters. I even held a spot outside a local café, on the street—open to anyone—to chat about whatever they wanted to chat about.

I came to realize I had to go back to face what I had run away from. I was not at peace. My old priest friend was now dead, but when I walked up the hill to the old presbytery, I felt the ghosts. It was a different time. Priests had some *permission* to open the skeletons in their closets.

**Listening to message from his body**

**Renewed connection to that "something bigger"**

I accessed this help and for the next years, up to now, I have been working on a very select mission to provide ways for young priests to undergo a more personal discernment process as to their emotional well-being. We work outside the Institution, but we are not against that Institution either. It is another moment of coming home, although this time, I have a much deeper sense of what belonging to God means.

I serve still. I love. And society is more accepting now too—I think a tad wiser when it comes to realizing that a priest is not a stand-in for God. This is still a dilemma: How to help people see the humanity in their clergy, and how to help clergy see the godliness in people. We don't do our work in private, but it is often privately sought.

Where am I now? I have never taken on another parish. I don't even imagine one would take me on! I am still available to guide the hearts and souls of young priests. They are entering a Church that has been disgraced by its unwillingness, in the beginning anyway, to acknowledge the deep harm that has been done.

But something else is calling me to go back to South America again. I fancy my self able to help begin a theological school there, or at least a local community. I have become more of the Jesuit following. Could I take that and be a gateway for the young men there—disenfranchised by poverty, drawn to power through horrendous crime? Are there new people there who can see beyond this, perhaps even a young priest or clergy?

When I was a boy, I had an innocent desire to be part of something bigger. I have been part of such things. I have found safe places. But what I seek now is bigger than an institution—even an Institution as old, big, and powerful as the Catholic Church. I don't think badly of institutions, but I am deeply saddened by how disconnected they can become from people who just hunger for a God that is unwrapped. Perhaps that is the bigger thing I want to be part of now: to help people unwrap God. This is a very different kind of service.

I don't know if I will go back to my last parish in South America. Perhaps it [the parish] just needs to finish its own story. I wonder what happened to little Samuel and his friends? Did I leave anything with them that they remember, that helped them grow into young men? I'm willing to wait on this decision a bit longer.

I am eighty-two years old now. Maybe I will go there and sit down in the dirt where I will die. I have no family left here; the Church has long since passed being my family. It's peculiar to be eighty-two and looking again for what bigger thing I am to be part of next. Maybe that will always be my quest.

**Postscript**: Patrick did go back to South America, but not to start a school. In his will, however, he requested that his personal earnings be used to build a legacy that speaks to his unfinished work with young boys—to raise a new generation of men who can know something beyond poverty and despair.

# Arriving at our Beginning and Knowing its Place in Us

## I have always known this place . . .

*This final chapter was written on the grounds of sacred sites in England.*

I began this book with the haunting words of T.S. Eliot:

> *"We shall not cease from exploration and the end of all*
> *our exploring will be to arrive where we started*
> *and know the place for the first time."*[1]

I re-member now; I have always known this place. It is the innocent energy I felt as a child on my parents' farm every time I dug my hands and feet into the raw earth. It is the orientation to Life that has infused my choice of profession, my teaching, and my care for others. It is the place of deep belonging that holds me still as I travel across the globe.

What I have learned is that:

> *Life alone does not present and create this experience of*
> *deep belonging for me. It is I, turning toward and opening*
> *to Life, maturing in my capacity to work with what is*
> *addressing me, that continues to refresh, deepen and*
> *expand how I come to experience that Life.*

There, I know my origin in Life's nature and its place in me. This is my most personal union with what touches, calls, and capacitates me to live.

During my experience of writing this book, I have been reminded of how tender and personal this inner call to return and re-member is. I came back to walk in the land of my ancestral spirits. I sat in the darkness of Little Gidding,[2] and as the ancient church bell tolled through the cold, windy night, I felt the comfort of its call to emptiness. I gazed into the depths of the decaying pool at Burnt Norton[3] and felt the tender movements of renewed promise as the air danced with the leaves and the earth pushed fragile but stubborn Life through the old, hardened barrier. I became joyfully still.

I explored the rolling landform and watched the ebb and flow of the surf as one movement led into another. I inspected what my way of living so far had washed up onto the beach. My sense of connection to all that is alive has been renewed and expanded. I see clearer what it means, what it is going to demand of me, to care about all that aspires to live.

Preston suggests that our dark nights, our experiences of angst and seeking autonomy, are "necessary as a means of human discipline . . . to [be brought back to our] deeper spiritual union."[4]

*We participate in this larger spiritual story through*
*the patterns of our personal leadership roles that we*
*take up in our will to learn discipline.*

*What matters is not so much the patterns, events,*
*and attachments themselves.*

*Rather, as Eliot says, the purpose is revealed in what*
*those events and attachments have stood for.*

Time, he says, gives us not only the *experience* of Life but also the *meaning* of what exists in Life.

I see all the ways I have tried to stay connected to what, in truth, is simple. The complexity has come from my need to limit truth to what I needed it to be. I continue to learn how to trust Life's presence with me. It is about suspending effort when the challenge is to listen and let the important things—what matters—emerge.

The movement between complexity and simplicity is one of the cycles of coming to live fully. I am also reminded of the cycle of decay and rebirth, of the need to put aside old ways so new ones can grow. I've witnessed the emergence and fading of the seasons of my life. Touching the fragility of the dying rose, even as the breeze rustled about it, reassured me that the presence of Life never leaves, it only transforms.

I believe that you and me, and others around us, have this ability to realize the potential of the Life force that we are and that we originate in.

*It has been said that we each have our route to Little Gidding—*
*to that need to be emptied of untruths in order to be*
*awakened and sustained by the evolution of deeper truths.*

Taking hold of and leading with the authority that Life gives means we can creatively encounter the dilemmas that Life in the midst of human experience brings.

On a day-to-day level, this means never surrendering our search for the truths that our dilemmas reveal. In allowing our lives to be vessels for the greater, transformative work of Life's creation, our evolving maturity will open the way for something that matters to future generations.

Believing that we can find meaning in and grow through what we face doesn't dismiss the suffering that continues to inflict pain through the ravages of poverty, prolonged abuse, and denial of human rights. Rather, facing truth and staying connected to it makes us mindful, as Buddhist teaching suggests, of what right action might come from that truth.

This is not an easy way. It demands that we take the time to look deeper. It means admitting that we cannot squeeze any more out of a parched life, that we must be the first one to step away from what is finished and step toward what opens us and our world to Life again.

To live is to know courage—the courage to keep seeking that convergence between the creative nature that we are and the truths of Life we are here to discover. It is in this *stillpoint*[5] of unending and renewed striving to unearth and re-member meaning into our lives that Life in itself becomes enough.

# Notes

## Prelude

1. *Life* as an expansive and sacred force is distinguished from our everyday experiences of life events and choices. This force has its own inherent will to preserve itself. We, as creative matter of, and vessels for, this force know congruence and aliveness in it when we turn and open our selves to what is being asked.

2. Viktor Frankl, *Man's Search for Meaning* (New York, NY: Washington Square Press, originally published in1959), 131. Print. It was Viktor Frankl who reminded us that, "Ultimately, man should not ask what the meaning of his life is, but rather he must recognize that it is *he* who is asked. In a word, each man is questioned by life; he can only answer to life by answering for his own life."

3. To *see* through a deeper and spiritual (versus precursory) lens is to see into how the breath and spirit of Life touches and moves what is beyond our pre-conceived human notions, assumptions, and, even, abilities. It requires that we empty our selves and bear witness to the ways we all seek and garner the courage to open to these intense and very personal movements.

4. Stephen Evans, *Soren Kierkegaard's Christian Psychology: Insight for Counseling and Pastoral Care* (Vancouver, BC: Regent College Publishing, 1990), 43. Print.

5. "Small self" describes the childlike stage of development wherein we reach to others to be the holders of our security, the mirrors of our identity, where the world exists as an object to meet our immediate needs. Ideally, we mature in our capacity to trust that our internal safety, our inherent value, originates in a source greater than our caregivers, separate even from any actions we undertake to secure our value and human identity. Experiencing both the limits and complexities inherent in human existence, we begin to accept that purposes beyond our singular needs and vision, exist. We mature, or not, in our willingness to relax into this greater essence and to trust being held by it.

6. In keeping with the existential-spiritual view that while leadership is not sourced within the individual, individuals carry the responsibility for making choices that align, within them selves, the presence and purpose of source

with personal context. This integration of context and choice is one's personal way of leadership. Values, beliefs, emotional responses, and behavioural choices serve as entry points wherein we can see where we are, including what may need to be realigned. The progressive discernment of congruence is where the personal leadership process keeps our sense of call alive, current, and purposeful.

## Early Roots of a Very Personal Call

1. Max Ehrmann, *Desiderata* (Written and copyrighted in 1929). Retrieved from http://www.sapphyr.net/largegems/desiderata.htm. Web. 13 Feb. 2009.

2. Milton Mayeroff, *On Caring* (New York, NY: Harper Perennial, 1971), 53. Print.

3. Elisabeth Roudinesco, *Why Psychoanalysis?* (New York, NY: Columbia University Press, 2001), 3. Print.

4. Nisargadatta, quoted in Helen Exley, *Timeless Values* (Great Britain: Helen Exley Giftbooks, 2002). Print.

## Living our Truth and Staying in the Flow of Life

1. Paul K. Kramer, *Redeeming time* (citing from Eliot's original work in the poem "The Dry Salvages," Plymouth, UK: Cowley Publications, 2007), 114. Print.

2. Charles M. Johnston, *Necessary Wisdom* (Seattle, WA: ICD Press, 1991), 128. Print.

3. Kramer, *Redeeming time*, 108.

4. Kramer, *Redeeming time*, 109.

5. T.S. Eliot, *Four Quartets* (London, UK: Faber and Faber Limited, 1944), 53. Print.

# Personal Leadership: A Process of Growing and Re-membering

1. Paul Maiteny and Bruce Reed, "Oscillation: A Meaning and Values-centered Approach to Sustainability of Human Systems" (Paper presented at the International Sociological Association's XIV World Congress, 'Social knowledge: Heritage, challenges, perspectives,' WG01 Sociocybernetics & Social Systems Theory, Montreal: 26 July, 1998), 10.

2. Mahatma Ghandi. Retrieved from http://www.brainyquote.com. Web 24 July 2009.

3. Jack Kornfield, *A Path with Heart* (New York, NY: Bantam Books, 1993). Print.

4. Eliot, *Four Quartets*.

5. *Shadow* is a psychological term used to describe that "place" (in our own unconsciousness, projected onto another person or thing) where we put what we do not yet feel capacitated to own, to face, certainly to grow.

6. Mayeroff, *On Caring*, 50.

7. Ehrmann, *Desiderata*.

8. Martin Buber, *I and Thou* (New York, NY: Simon and Schuster, 1970), 57. Print.

9. Margaret Wheatley, *Turning to One Another* (San Francisco, CA: Berrett-Koehler Publishers, Inc., 2002), 82. Print.

10. Buber, *I and Thou*, 159.

11. Buber, *I and Thou*, 70.

12. Parker Palmer, *A Hidden Wholeness: The Journey Toward an Undivided Life* (San Francisco, CA: Jossey-Bass, 2004), 175. Print.

13. Palmer, *A Hidden Wholeness: The Journey Toward an Undivided Life*, 127.

14. Eliot, *Four Quartets*, 53.

# Arriving at our Beginning and Knowing its Place in Us

1. Eliot, *Four Quartets*, 43.

2. "Little Gidding" is both the last poem in T.S. Eliot's famous collection of poems *Four Quartets*, and an actual place—a tiny parish in the district of Cambridgeshire, north of London, England. There is a tiny chapel on the property dating back to the early 1600s, which, though inspired by Nicholas Ferrar, was led by a community of pastors from various denominations. Its simplicity and starkness is meant to invite pilgrims to empty themselves of preoccupations, to enter deep contemplative stillness with the natural world. In this emptying, it is believed that the "tongues of fire" test motives—fire being the symbol of purification.

3. "Burnt Norton" is the name of T.S. Eliot's first poem in the *Four Quartets* series. It was named after an old English manor that still stands today and is located west of London. Eliot came upon it one day while exploring the countryside with his lady friend and was intrigued by its expansiveness and beauty. It symbolized for him that first and primary relationship between the logos (transcendent time) and real-time of physical life. Here, the element and movement of air re-members us to the flow in our primal beingness. Here, we are reminded to step back and experience the immediacy of the moment where spirit infuses our present with all that has been and can be.

4. R. Preston, *"Four Quartets" Rehearsed* (London: Sheed and Ward, 1946), vi. Print.

5. Eliot, *Four Quartets*, 17. Print. Eliot used the phrase "at the still point of the turning world" to describe those unutterable moments when we sense the stream of eternity present shaping and molding what is coming into being now.

# Acknowledgments

I wish first to acknowledge the deeply meaningful works of T.S. Eliot, particularly his poetic renderances of nature's movements in the *Four Quartets*. They have served in a major way to bring me back to that place where I could re-member what stirs, moves, and dances in me still.

I recall the cold October day when you picked me up from the bus stop, Christine, to help me find my way to the tiny parish of Little Gidding—in particular, the quiet space of Ferrar House. I felt invited into the warmth of this historic refuge by the hot meal, the heater by my bed. Your courage to pierce the cold, windy night and ring the ancient bell ministered to my soul.

I remember you, Tony and Jenny, from Little Gidding Bed and Breakfast in the English Cotswolds. You cared enough to bring me to the inspirational place of Burnt Norton, one of the places T.S. Eliot wrote of. There, I indeed sensed how the element of air moved through what resides in place. I remember to this day the experience of walking with you both in the garden, even as we each took our own place in it.

The stewards of Ocklynge Manor on the English coastline offered space for me to sit quietly, to sense both the legendary spirit of the place and the words that were ready to be written.

I thank each of you who told your story here. You trusted that your experiences of learning could inspire others to live what matters to them. How you've lived what is yours is touching and encouraging others to stay open to what is unfolding in their lives.

Yvon, you are indeed my partner in Life. I am grateful for your presence with me and in my Life work.

How does one thank Life for its unwavering commitment and presence? Perhaps just that I pledge to return to it its honor and its purpose in me.

CPSIA information can be obtained
at www.ICGtesting.com
Printed in the USA
LVOW05s0355290118
564359LV00017B/71/P